Maths Inside and Out

For the Early Years Foundation Stage

Anna Skinner

Acknowledgements

The author would like to thank the staff and children at Ridgeway Primary and Nursery School, Croydon, and in particular

Helen Burns
Anna House
Joanna Redzimski
Nicola Selby, Manor Park Primary School, Sutton,
and Carole Skinner

Thanks also to the following:

Angela Beall, Bardsey Primary School, Leeds
Louise Glover, Bentley Drive JMI School, Walsall
Lynwen Barnsley, Education Effectiveness, Swansea
Andrea Trigg, Felbridge Primary School, West Sussex
Ed Humble, Hampton Wick Infant and Nursery School, Teddington
Emma Kneller, Melody Makers, Gloucestershire
Father Rudolf Loewenstein, St Christina's Primary School, Camden
Elizabeth Wyles, St John's Priory School, Banbury
Kate Joiner, Stroud School, Hampshire
Sharon Sutton, University of Reading
Helen Elis Jones, University of Wales, Bangor
Rachel Richards, Send C of E First School, Surrey
Deborah de Gray, West Kingsdown CE Primary School, Kent

The BEAM Development Group:

Joanne Barrett, Rotherfield Primary School, Islington
Mark Day, Hanover Primary School, Islington
Catherine Horton, St Jude and St Paul's, Islington
Simone de Juan, Prior Weston Primary School, Islington

Published by BEAM Education
Maze Workshops
72a Southgate Road
London N1 3JT

Telephone 020 7684 3323
Fax 020 7684 3334
Email info@beam.co.uk
www.beam.co.uk

© BEAM Education 2008,
    a division of Nelson Thornes

Reprinted in 2009

ISBN 978 1 9062 2440 0
British Library Cataloguing-in-Publication Data
Data available
Edited by Marion Dill
Design and layout by Reena Kataria
Illustrations by Annabel Hudson
Printed by Graphycems, Spain

Contents

Maths Inside and Out

Introduction

We all know that the best way for children to understand maths is to use their interest and curiosity in the world around them as a springboard. We also know that play underpins learning, and we want our children to be actively involved in a whole range of different experiences to get the most from the environments we create.

The activities in *Maths Inside and Out* gives children opportunities to play, run, jump, create and manipulate materials, make choices, invent more problems and talk about their solutions. You will find that the suggested activities and experiences build on children's individual enthusiasm and provide a mathematical curriculum that is child led. This type of challenging curriculum is so much richer than one in which children just listen to us adults explaining things. In setting up these experiences, there are opportunities for all children to choose, create, change and be part of a stimulating environment with lots of opportunities for you and them to be versatile, to experiment and to extend and enhance their learning.

As organisation and space in every early years centre and classroom are unique, I have focused on the two big spaces that everyone has: indoors and outside. Focusing on planning for these two spaces together and making connections between the different areas of play opens up a wealth of additional learning opportunities. Outside, children can work on a much bigger scale, make more noise and use larger body movements. There is space for them to use larger tools such as real paint rollers and full-size balls. Inside, there is scope to stimulate experiences and support children's ideas and interests as well as showing them how to use different maths tools and resources.

For both of these two large spaces, inside and outside, I have suggested six themed areas that could be part of your continuous provision or function at different times throughout the year. These are areas where you can organise opportunities to play, provide resources and space, give children time to explore, support them making choices and provide yourself with an opportunity

to observe the children and, most importantly, where you can enhance the maths experiences for all of the children.

Every workshop chapter opens by identifying the maths that the children will experience during play, with an emphasis on problem solving. There are suggestions for additional and specific resources to collect together that will enhance the area. For instance, in the art space there are details of the range of paints and papers that will make it into a very workable workshop area. In addition, there are suggested books and stories to read that reflect the theme as well as music for everyone to listen to and songs to sing along to. You will notice that there are ideas on how to use technology to support maths learning and also what every area needs, which is a maths toolkit of equipment to support the learning.

The individual activity pages for each area identify the maths learning and the vocabulary that you need to use and emphasise. They give good starting points for discussions with the children. I have suggested questions to ask that will encourage children and give them confidence to believe that they can do things themselves or refer them to other children who may be able to help.

Above all, the activities will stimulate and support children's own ideas. Leave time in a discussion for children's reflections and comments, as this will shape your response to the look, listen, note comments that you find with each activity.

What this book provides is lots of ideas, games and activities to enhance and support many different maths learning journeys. You can tailor all the experiences to the needs of individual children, who all deserve first-hand experiences that reflect their interests. I hope you and your children have as much fun and laughter doing the activities as I and the children in my nursery class experienced.

About this book

Topic and introduction

There are 12 chapters in this book, each one focusing on one of the 12 themed areas, six indoors and six outside. The workshop activities are intended to be play based, and once you have explained and modelled the language, children develop their own ideas.

Maths learning chart

This chart identifies the maths in each of the activities in that chapter. The seven maths strands in the renewed Primary Framework have been amalgamated in this chart to reflect the maths organisation of the Early Years Foundation Stage.

Problem solving identified

This chart reflects the aspects of the using and applying strand of the renewed Primary Framework where the progression in communication, reasoning, enquiry and problem solving is identified.

Sports centre

A sports centre workshop supports children's developing climbing, balancing and throwing skills. A climbing frame makes a wonderful centrepiece for a sports centre, where, over time, you can add different pieces of equipment such as skipping ropes and hoops as an extension. Using the outdoor area for lots of running, jumping and hopping along huge number tracks, for example, is a good way to engage children in exploring maths learning on a large scale.

Maths learning chart

Maths content

Activities	Page	Number	Calculating	Shape and space	Measures	Problem solving
Pathway hop	84	✿				✿
Sorting out the balls	85	✿				✿
Ten-pin bowling	86			✿		✿
Goals	87			✿		
Circuit training	88			✿	✿	✿
Lifting weights	89				✿	✿

Problem solving identified

Activities

Problem solving	Pathway hop	Sorting out the balls	Ten-pin bowling	Goals	Circuit training	Lifting weights
Solving problems		✿	✿		✿	✿
Representing	✿		✿	✿	✿	
Decision making		✿				✿
Reasoning		✿				✿
Communicating	✿				✿	

Resourcing

These are only some of the resources that children can use. To encourage independence, make sure the resources are readily accessible.

Developing a learning conversation

Give children time to think through their ideas and consolidate or reflect on what they know by asking one of the open-ended questions or statements suggested.

Using ICT

Here, you find ideas for extending the mathematical learning with technology as well as providing children with the opportunity to develop ICT skills.

Maths toolkit

A maths toolkit in every area of your setting will support children as they solve problems. It should be easily available to them and could contain different types of measuring tapes, counters, number lines and tracks.

Books to read

Suggestions for storybooks and picture books linked to the area. Add factual books and magazines and motivate children's interests by reading some of the stories or making up stories together.

Songs

Traditional and modern songs and rhymes to incorporate into the activity

Music

Young children love all sorts of music, and the suggested pieces will have them dancing, clapping, stomping and counting the beat ...

Making the most of your sports centre

Resourcing the sports centre

Encourage the group to help collect resources for the sports centre: a range of different-sized balls, quoits, hoops, skittles skipping ropes; beanbags; climbing equipment, tunnels, benches, floor mats; bats, goal nets, parachutes, ladders.

Developing a learning conversation

I wonder if it is possible to make a square shape with a skipping rope?
What can we do to remember how many star jumps you can do?
Can you think of a way to make a walkway across the sports centre?

Using ICT to support maths

Video camera to create an action highlights film
Calculator programmed to be a repeating counter
Stopwatch to time how long it takes
to do pigeon steps from one area to the next

Maths toolkit

Stopwatches, sand timers, measuring tapes, number cards, score boards, magnetic board and numbers, number tracks and lines, interlocking cubes, white board and marker pen

Books to read

Cat Among the Cabbages by Alison Bartlett (Gullane Children's Books)
Hit the Ball, Duck by Jez Alborough (Harper Collins)
Goal! by Colin McNaughton (Harper Collins)

Songs to sing

Head, shoulders, knees and toes
One finger, one thumb, keep moving
Hokey cokey
If you're happy and you know it, clap your hands

Music to listen to

Let's Get Started by the Black Eyed Peas
Brandenberg Concerto No 1 by Johann Sebastian Bach
We are the Champions by Queen

Sports centre 83

Using the activity pages

Main activity

The main activities in *Maths Inside and Out* cover a range of mathematical experiences. You can use the activities flexibly to accommodate the requirements of the children in your setting.

Things to ask

Open-ended questions stimulate children's thought processes and encourage the use of mathematical vocabulary. We have given three sample questions for each activity.

Look, listen, note

This section gives you ideas of what to look out for when you assess the children's mathematical understanding as well as their personal and social development.

Challenge

Here, you find suggestions for extending or varying the activity for older or more able children.

Marine biologist

Children use small aquarium nets to catch plastic sea creatures that are in a large fish tank or water tray. They analyse what creatures they have netted and sort them into a sorting tray. When they have categorised, counted and discussed the creatures, children put them back into the tank.

You need

- A large selection of plastic sea creatures including fish, crabs, sea horses, in a fish tank or water tray
- An aquarium net for each child
- Sorting trays

Things to ask

Why do you think you have more fish than sea horses?
Can you guess how many dolphins you have got altogether?
How can we find out the total number of fish you collected?

Look, listen, note

Which children can
- sort the creatures into different groups?
- discuss differences between each group?
- use the language of calculation?

Challenge

Children record the results of each sorting and compare the differences.

Children re-sort the sea creatures, using different criteria.

Words to use

one, two, three ... ten, how many?, total, more, less, fewer, altogether, same, different, sort

Maths learning

Calculating

Classifying by organising and arranging

Knowing that a group of things changes when something is added

Using language such as 'more' or 'less'

102 Maths Inside and Out

Jewel collector

Arrange a collection of costume jewellery, beads and gems on a large piece of velvet. Give children magnifying lenses to examine the jewels. They then take it in turns to choose a number card and put that many jewels in each box. The next child changes the number of jewels in the boxes according to the number on their card by either removing some jewels or adding to the collection. When the game is over, children choose a soft toy to dress in jewels.

You need
- Costume jewellery, beads and gems
- A large piece of velvet
- Magnifying lenses
- Three jewellery boxes
- 1–5 number cards
- Soft toys

Things to ask
How many jewels are in each of the boxes?
Do you need to take some jewels away or add some?
How can you find out how many jewels there are altogether?

Look, listen, note
Which children can
- use words such as 'more' or 'less' when playing the game?
- work out how many more or fewer jewels they need to put in the box?
- suggest ways of finding a total?

Challenge
Children start with a larger number of jewels and jewellery boxes.
Children use 1–8 number cards.

Words to use
one, two three ... five, how many?, more, less, altogether, add, take

Maths learning
Calculating
Comparing two groups of objects
Adding and taking away from a group of objects
Counting out objects from a larger group

Real world 103

Small-world workshop

A child-friendly, inspirational, small-world workshop can produce high-quality play experiences. This workshop area works particularly well if it is set up as a backdrop to small-world play such as an underground cave for sea creatures, rather than only being a resource area for small-world equipment. A planned small-world area provides opportunities for children to rehearse maths skills such as counting and sorting and supports children who are cooperating with each other in play.

Maths learning chart

Maths content

Activities	Page	Number	Calculating	Shape and space	Measures	Problem solving
Going on an outing	12	✿				✿
Frogs in the pond	13	✿		✿		✿
Sharing in pairs	14		✿			✿
Feely-bag line-up	15		✿			✿
Making an animal house	16			✿	✿	✿
Freezing cold dinosaurs	17			✿	✿	✿

Problem solving identified

Activities

Problem solving	Going on an outing	Frogs in the pond	Sharing in pairs	Feely-bag line-up	Making an animal house	Freezing cold dinosaurs
Solving problems	✿	✿		✿	✿	
Representing			✿			
Decision making	✿	✿		✿	✿	✿
Reasoning			✿	✿	✿	✿
Communicating			✿	✿		✿

Making the most of your small-world workshop

Resourcing the workshop

Encourage the group to help collect resources for the small-world workshop: play people; train set, fire/police station, garage and vehicles, road and cars, boats and harbour, castle and knights, kings and queens, wooden village; sea creatures and fish, farm and farmyard animals, jungle and wild animals; doll's house and furniture; floor mats.

Developing a learning conversation

I wonder which furniture will fit in the little house?

How could we design a car park for the cars?

What could we use to make a ladder for the fire engine?

Using ICT to support maths

Programmable toy to take messages and make journeys for the characters

Computer and storybook program to watch

Electric circuits to provide lighting for scenarios

Maths toolkit

Number tiles, number cards, number line, dice

Books to read

Oi! Get off our Train by John Burningham (Red Fox Picture Books)

Duck in the Truck by Jez Alborough (Picture Lions)

Harry and the Bucketful of Dinosaurs by Ian Whybrows (Picture Puffin)

Mrs Armitage, Queen of the Road by Quentin Blake (Jonathan Cape)

Songs to sing

Old Macdonald

Row, row, row the boat

1, 2, 3, 4, 5, once I caught a fish alive

Down in the jungle

Music to listen to

Peter and the Wolf by Sergei Prokofiev

The Nutcracker Suite by Piotr Tchaikovsky

Going on an outing

Give everyone a bus stop and 10 small-world people to line up in a queue. The children take it in turns to roll the dice, say the number and put that many people on the bus. After three turns, each child counts how many people are still in their bus queue. The child with most people is the winner.

Things to ask

Does anyone have a girl with stripy socks first in their queue?

How many people did you put on the bus this time?

Can you say how you knew how many people were in your queue?

Look, listen, note

Which children can

- identify who is first and last in their queue?
- say the dice number as they take their turn?
- count their characters correctly?

Challenge

Children use a 1–6 dice and more characters to play the game.

Change the rule so that the winner of the game is the child with fewest people after three rolls of the dice.

Words to use

one, two, three … ten, count, how many?, number, first, last, second, third

Maths learning

Number

Saying and using number names

Counting reliably to 10 objects

Using ordinal numbers

Frogs in the pond

Children turn over a number card from a shuffled 1–3 pack. They say the number and collect that many frogs from the box. When they have collected all the frogs, children release them into the wild by arranging them in the 'pond'.

You need

- A shallow tray half filled with water
- Small rocks, stones and moss to make a environment in the tray
- 12 small cards with a number from 1 to 3 written on and shuffled
- 20 plastic frogs in a small box

Things to ask

I wonder how many frogs are in your collection?

How can we find out how many frogs you are going to release into the pond?

Have you decided whereabouts in the pond you will put that frog?

Look, listen, note

Which children can

- recognise and say some number names?
- describe where they are going to put their frog, using positional words?
- count accurately the number of frogs in their collection?

Challenge

Children turn over the number cards, remove that many frogs from the pond and count how many they have rescued altogether.

Children play the game with more frogs and a 1–6 dice.

Words to use

one, two, three, how many?, how many altogether?, count, next to, beside, in front of, behind, in the pond, on top of

Maths learning

Number and shape and space

Using some number names

Counting reliably to 10 objects

Using positional language

Sharing in pairs

Put a large collection of different objects such as play people, building blocks, coins, counters, buttons and cotton-wool balls in a wicker basket. Ask pairs of children to put a scoopful each in a small basket or container and then share the objects between them. When they have shared about 20 objects, each child takes their own collection, sorts it into small baskets and labels them.

Things to ask

How do you know that you have both got the same number of objects?

How many objects do you think you have altogether?

Do you think you shared fairly?

Look, listen, note

Which children can

- find a way of sharing the objects?
- explain how they know they have the same number of objects?
- estimate how many objects they have altogether?

Challenge

Children record how many objects they started with as well as the result after they have shared them.

Children use the small-world objects to share among four soft toys.

Maths learning

Calculating

Comparing two groups of objects

Finding the total number of items in two groups

Sharing objects into two equal groups

Feely-bag line-up

Line up 10 sea creatures on the seashore. Children choose five to put in the sea cave. Everyone counts them by feeling without taking them out of the cave and agrees there are five. They put a '5' number card next to the line of sea creatures. Children take it in turns to spin the spinner and either put 'one more' in the cave or take one sea creature out of the cave for 'one less'. Each time, they change the number card to record the new amounts on the seashore. Children have two turns each and then estimate how many sea creatures are in the cave before tipping them out and checking by counting.

Things to ask

Can you explain how you knew how many were in the cave?

If we take one out of the cave, how many will there be then?

I'm not sure if we need to change the number card. What do you think?

Look, listen, note

Which children can

- estimate how many objects are in the cave?
- suggest the appropriate number card?
- explain how many are left in the cave after one object has been removed?

Challenge

Use a spinner labelled 'two more' and 'two less'.

Children work out how many are on the sea shore if there are six sea creatures in the cave.

Words to use

one, two, three … ten, one more, one less, altogether, total, more, fewer

Maths learning

Calculating

Finding the total number of items in a group by counting

Finding 'one more' or 'one less' than a number

Using the language of adding and subtracting

Making an animal house

Children choose a farm animal and a small box. They measure and cut up pieces of fabric and papers and glue them onto the sides of the box. They fill their covered boxes with straw and sit their animal in the box.

Things to ask

Will your animal fit easily into your box?

Can you say something about the shape of your box?

How did you decide what size to cut the material?

Look, listen, note

Which children can

- say why they choose that size or shape box?
- explain how they know whether their animal will fit in the box?
- explain how they made their animal house?

Challenge

Children add handles to turn their animal box into a carry box.

Children use a different-shaped box and make a pet animal house.

Words to use

big, small, long, short, size, square, rectangle, edge, corner

Maths learning

Shape and space and measures

Using mathematical words to describe shape and size

Understanding variations in size

Describing solutions to practical problems

Freezing cold dinosaurs

Freeze small-world dinosaurs in coloured water using different-sized plastic pots. Remove the ice blocks from the containers and put them into shallow trays. Children use gloves to handle the ice blocks and discuss what is frozen inside them. They talk about the different shapes and sizes of the blocks and use tapes to measure them. The children guess which dinosaur will appear from the ice first.

You need

- Dinosaurs or other small-world characters
- A selection of different-sized plastic pots
- Coloured water
- Shallow trays
- Gloves
- Measuring tapes

Things to ask

How can we find out which ice block is the tallest?

I wonder how we can describe the shape of the blocks?

What's happening to the ice?

Look, listen, note

Which children can

- suggest which is the tallest or the smallest ice block?
- describe any shape features of the ice blocks?
- compare different properties of the ice blocks as they melt?

Challenge

Using different kinds of timer, children time how long it takes for an ice block to melt and the dinosaur to escape.

Children make more ice blocks, using different-shaped containers.

Words to use

round, wide, tall, short, taller than, shorter than, square, rectangle, cube, cylinder

Maths learning

Shape and space and measures

Observing shapes and comparing sameness and difference

Using the language of measurement

Using mathematical names for shapes

Art space

An art space is an exciting, creative area for children to work in. It is much more than a painting table: it is an area where children can access different tools and media to explore and develop their own interests and where they can experiment with various types of materials.

Maths learning chart

Maths content

Activities	Page	Number	Calculating	Shape and space	Measures	Problem solving
Wall hangings	20	✿			✿	✿
Revealing	21	✿			✿	✿
Rolling flowers	22		✿	✿		✿
Mirror designs	23		✿	✿		✿
Metal sculptures	24			✿		✿
Ice-cube painting	25			✿		✿

Problem solving identified

Problem solving	Wall hangings	Revealing	Rolling flowers	Mirror designs	Metal sculptures	Ice-cube painting
Solving problems	✿	✿	✿		✿	✿
Representing				✿	✿	
Decision making	✿	✿	✿			
Reasoning	✿	✿				
Communicating				✿		✿

Making the most of your art space

Resourcing the art space

Encourage the group to help collect resources for the art space: a range of different types of paints, brushes in various sizes, washing line, drying rack, water pots, palettes; paper in various sizes and colours and of different thickness; pens, crayons, pastels, chalks, charcoal; corks, masking tape, glue, paper plates, lolly sticks, rollers, fabrics, art straws, string, elastic bands, mirrors; natural objects such as fir cones, conkers, clay.

Developing a learning conversation

What did you decide was the best shape for your picture frame?

How could you change the shape of your clay pot?

Are there any problems with making a number print block that way?

Using ICT to support maths

Scanner to publish designs

Digital camera to record artwork

Computer drawing package

Maths toolkit

Rulers, measuring tapes, 2D and 3D shapes

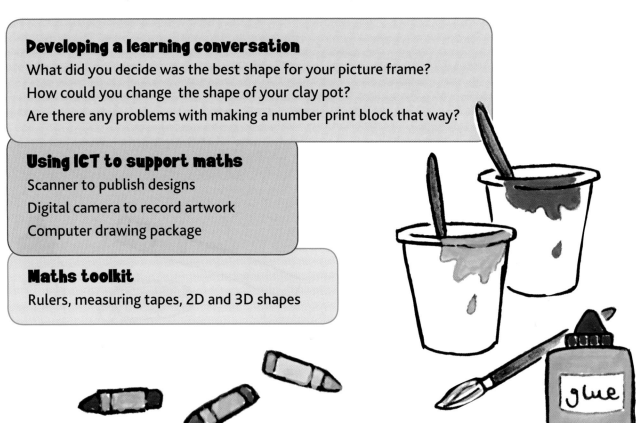

Books to read

Chidi Only Likes Blue: An African Book of Colours by Ifeoma Onyefulu (Frances Lincoln)

The Patchwork Quilt by Valerie Flournoy (Scholastic)

Elmer by David McKee (HarperCollins)

The Mixed-up Chameleon by Eric Carle (Crowell)

Songs to sing

I can sing a rainbow

Colour my world

Music to listen to

Rhapsody on a Theme of Paganini by Sergei Rachmaninoff

Music for the Royal Fireworks by George Frideric Handel

Wall hangings

Children make 10 streamers of different lengths that they cut from various ribbons and fabrics. They glue the streamers to a plant stick and tie string at either end so that the stick can be suspended from a washing line across the room.

You need

- A selection of different types of ribbons, including silk, velvet, sequinned and wrapping ribbons, string and wool
- A plant stick for each child
- String
- Scissors
- Glue
- A washing line
- Tape measures
- Rulers

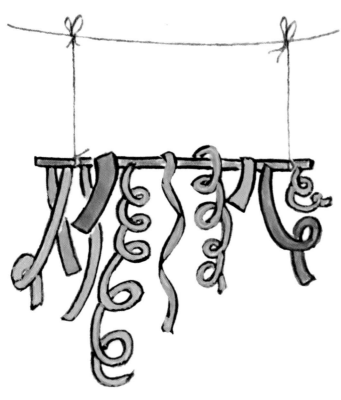

Things to ask

How many more ribbons do you need to choose?

I wonder which of your 10 ribbons is the longest?

Can you explain how you measured your ribbons?

Look, listen, note

Which children can

- count the ribbons accurately?
- explain a strategy for measuring the ribbons?
- identify the longest and the shortest ribbons?

Challenge

Children make a circular mobile using different materials.

Children find a way of hanging lots of different numbers from a plant stick.

Words to use

one, two, three ... ten, how many?, more, less, long, longer, longest, short, shorter, shortest

Maths learning

Number and measures

Counting 10 everyday objects

Ordering items by length

Knowing that numbers identify how many are in a set

Revealing

Children cut five different lengths of masking tape, number them and stick them in different positions on a piece of card. They use various paint colours to roller over the card, including the masking tape. When the paint is dry, they peel off the masking tape to reveal the design.

You need
- Masking tape
- Measuring tapes
- Scissors
- Glue
- Cards
- Paints in various colours
- Rollers

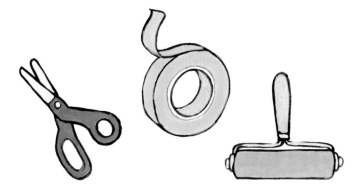

Things to ask

Can you say which piece of tape you stuck down first?
Where did you place your longest piece of masking tape?
What can you say about your design?

Look, listen, note

Which children can
- identify the order in which they stuck the tapes?
- identify the longest and the shortest pieces of masking tape?
- use ordinal language?

Challenge

Children create another design using a different number of tape lengths.

Children organise an exhibition of all the designs.

Words to use

one, two, three … five, first, second, third, last long, longer, longest, short, shorter, shortest

Maths learning

Number and measures
Saying and using number names
Recognising numerals
Ordering two or three items by length

Rolling flowers

The children arrange five picked flowers such as dandelions, daffodils or daisies (depending on the season, a mixture is best) on a large sheet of paper. They then choose one or two more flowers to add to their design. When they are happy with it, children cover the flowers with another piece of paper and use rolling pins to roll over the covered flowers, pressing down hard. When they have rolled all the flowers, they remove the covering paper to see the design they have made.

Things to ask

How many flowers did you use altogether?

What direction will you roll the rolling pin?

I wonder what sort of pattern you are going to make?

Look, listen, note

Which children can

- count out the flowers and add more?
- discuss the directions they are using the rolling pin?
- talk about the position of their flowers?

Challenge

Children record the flowers they used.

Children write a zigzag book of pictorial instructions on how to roll flowers, numbering the steps.

Words to use

how many?, one more, two more, altogether, total, up, down, sideways, diagonally, next to, beside, underneath, above, repeat, upside down

Maths learning

Calculating and shape and space

Adding 'one more' to a total

Making an arrangement with objects

Using the language of shape

Mirror designs

Ask the children to arrange a selection of materials on a mirror tile to create a design. They identify and discuss the reflections in the mirror and the doubling effect it has on their design. When their design is finished, they take a digital photo. The children play with a selection of hinged mirrors, looking at the designs they have made.

You need

- A collection of natural objects such as seeds and leaves
- Materials such as sequins, transparent plastic shapes
- A mirror tile for each child
- A digital camera
- Hinged mirrors (made by joining two mirrors with sticky tape along one side)

Things to ask

Can you tell me about your design?

How many seeds did you use and how many can you see in the mirror?

Are there any parts of your design that look the same?

Look, listen, note

Which children can

- count the mirror reflections?
- point out similar features in their design?
- discuss shapes that they observe in their design?

Challenge

Children make a pattern using different materials.

Children explore patterns using kaleidoscopes.

Words to use

two, four, six, eight, same, reflection, double

Maths learning

Calculating and shape and space

Counting repeated groups

Creating symmetrical patterns

Identifying patterns and shapes

Metal sculptures

Children cut metal wire into various lengths and twist them into different shapes and designs, using modelling clay as a base and to make joins.

Things to ask

Can you tell me about the design of your sculpture?

Have you used curved and straight lines?

Are there any parts of your sculpture that are the same?

Look, listen, note

Which children can

- identify curved and straight lines?
- discuss any properties of shape?
- refer to any aspects of symmetry in the sculpture?

Challenge

Children draw and display their sculpture.

Children develop their design by adding extra features.

Words to use

shape, straight, curved, corners, long, longer, longest, short, shortest

Maths learning

Shape and space

Using the language of shape

Showing awareness of symmetry

Using own ideas to explore orientation and position

Ice-cube painting

The children line the base of a small shallow tray with paper and sprinkle a teaspoonful of powder paint over the paper. They put an ice cube in the tray and tip it from side to side so that it slides backward and forward across the paper, mixing with the powder paint to make a design. Children then remove the ice cube and leave the design to dry.

You need

- Shallow trays or containers
- Paper
- Teaspoons
- Powder paint
- Ice cubes

Things to ask

How will you manage to slide the ice cube across the paper?

Can you see any shapes in your design?

Are there any parts of your design that are the same?

Look, listen, note

Which children can

- identify symmetrical parts of their design?
- talk about aspects of their design by using shape words?
- describe how to manipulate their tray to move the ice cube?

Challenge

Children use several different colours of powder paint.

Children experiment with different-shaped trays and containers.

Words to use

up, down, side to side, straight line, triangle, square, corner, across, back, circle, spiral

Maths learning

Shape and space

Using the language of shape

Using everyday words to describe position

Showing awareness of symmetry

Newsroom

Writing areas sometimes known as graphic centres or offices are always popular with young children as they access pens, pencils and paper. Creating a newsroom gives children an opportunity to share their interests and the community news.

Maths learning chart

Maths content

Activities	Page	Number	Calculating	Shape and space	Measures	Problem solving
Number reference rolls	28	✿				✿
Glitter calculations	29	✿	✿			✿
Calculator numbers	30	✿				✿
Paper-clip chains	31	✿	✿		✿	✿
Projecting shapes game	32			✿		✿
Daily news	33			✿		✿

Problem solving identified

Activities

Problem solving	Number reference rolls	Glitter calculations	Calculator numbers	Paper-clip chains	Projecting shapes game	Daily news
Solving problems	✿		✿	✿	✿	✿
Representing		✿	✿	✿		✿
Decision making	✿	✿			✿	
Reasoning		✿			✿	
Communicating	✿	✿		✿		✿

Making the most of your newsroom

Resourcing the newsroom

Encourage the group to help collect resources for the newsroom: pens, pencils, pastels, chalks and boards, whiteboards and markers, crayons, charcoal; paper and card in various sizes, colours and shapes, wallpaper rolls, a supply of different-sized and -shaped envelopes; notepads, clipboards; assorted ready-made books, book-making materials, stapler, hole punch, treasury tags, paper clips, scissors, masking tape, sticky labels, glue sticks and sticky tape, computer keyboard, telephone; alphabet lines, name cards, message boxes, address labels, calendars, diaries.

Developing a learning conversation

How could you make your zigzag book longer?

Have you decided the best way to make an envelope?

Suppose you were numbering newspaper pages. What number would you start at?

Using ICT to support maths

Computer and writing program to write own stories and reviews

Scanner to scan own illustrations for stories

Maths toolkit

Number line, number cards, ruler, calendar, shapes, calculator

Songs to sing

Postman Pat

Alphabet song

Books to read

Dear Zoo by Rod Campbell (Campbell Books)

Dear Daddy by Philippe Dupasquier (Andersen)

Dr Seuss's ABC by Dr Seuss (Picture Lions)

In addition: newspapers, magazines, comics, storybooks, reference books

Music to listen to

Elite Syncopations by Scott Joplin

Piano Concerto B Flat Minor by Piotr Tchaikovsky

Number reference rolls

Explain to the children that they are going to make number reference rolls. Ask them to look through magazines to find and cut any numbers they see and stick it on one of the paper strips. When a strip has lots of numbers on, children tape the two ends together to make a continuous roll and suspend it on a broom handle. When the paper strips are all on the broom handle, children look for numbers in order.

Things to ask

How many numbers can you say?

What numbers have you cut out?

I wonder if there is a number larger than 8 on the roll?

Look, listen, note

Which children can

- recognise some numbers?
- identify strings of numbers?
- say some number sequences?

Challenge

Children use the number rolls to count backward.

Children make their own counting books.

Calculator numbers

Children glue headless matches or short tapers onto balsa wood or a polystyrene tray to make calculator number rubbing blocks. They make a block for each number, then make a rubbing of the number using thick paper and wax crayons. Children work together, putting the number rubbings in order and entering the numbers they made into the calculator.

You need

- Headless matches or short tapers
- Pieces of balsa wood or polystyrene trays
- PVC glue
- Thick paper
- Wax crayons
- Calculators

Things to ask

Can you rub a number larger than 3?

Has anyone rubbed their age number?

What number are you going to enter into the calculator?

Look, listen, note

Which children can

- recognise some calculator numbers?
- enter a number into the calculator?
- put the numbers in order?

Challenge

Children make a calculator number line.

Children make a rubbing of their house or flat number.

Words to use

one, two, three ... ten, numeral, calculator, number

Maths learning

Number

Using number names

Recognising numerals

Saying and using number names in order

Glitter calculations

Children use a tray of sand and glitter to record their calculations. They take it in turns to turn over a spotty number card and say the number. The rest of the group write the number 'one more' than the card number in their glitter trays. The card holder picks up the glitter counter, counts the spots on the card, adds the glitter counter to the number of spots and says the total. Everyone who wrote the correct number takes a large sequin. The first player to collect five sequins is the winner.

Things to ask

What number did you write in the sand?

How did you know that number was 'one more' than the card number?

Can you write the number 'one more' than 6?

Look, listen, note

Which children can

- say the number 'one more' than is on the card?
- include the counter when they count the spots?
- write the numbers in the sand tray?

Challenge

Children play the game writing 'one less', using a circle to cover up one of the spots.

Children write all the numbers they know in the sand.

Words to use

one, two, three ... ten, and, altogether, one more, total, enough, number

Maths learning

Number and calculating

Saying the number 'one more' than a given number

Counting to 10 objects

Writing numerals to 11

Paper-clip chains

Show the children how to connect together extra large paper clips to make a chain. Put a box of paper clips and a 1–3 dice on a tray. Children take it in turns to roll the dice, say the number and pick up that many paper clips. They thread the paper clips together until everyone has at least 10 joined paper clips or until they have used all the clips.

Things to ask

Have you collected more than 10 paper clips?

What numbers did you roll on the dice?

How did you know how many paper clips to pick up?

Look, listen, note

Which children can

- count out the paper clips from the box?
- name the number on the dice?
- talk about how many paper clips are on their chain?

Challenge

Children use a 1–6 dice.

Children compare their paper-clip chains and decide which is the longest.

Words to use

one, two, three ... ten, altogether, count, how many, total, more than, less than

Maths learning

Calculating

Finding the total number of items in two groups by counting

Relating addition to combining two groups of objects

Counting a specified number from a large group

Projecting shapes game

Children choose six 2D shapes from a collection of shapes in a box and arrange them on a table or on the floor. Put a shape on the overhead projector. They check if the shape that is reflected on the wall from the projector is the same as one of their shapes. If it is, they name it and put it back in the box. Each time you change the shape on the projector, children put back a shape if it is the same as one in their collection. Keep changing the shapes until all the shapes are back in the box.

You need

- An overhead projector
- A collection of 2D shapes in a box

Things to ask

Can you say something about the shapes you have chosen?

Why do you think that shape is a triangle?

What shape would you get if you put two squares together?

Look, listen, note

Which children can

- identify some of the properties of their shapes?
- say the names of the shapes they have chosen?
- refer to sameness and differences of their shapes?

Challenge

Children choose different shapes and put some together to make new shapes.

Children play the game, trying to keep the shapes.

Words to use

shape, corners, sides, square, rectangle, triangle, hexagon, circle

Maths learning

Shape and space

Matching shapes by recognising similarities

Selecting particular named shapes

Using the language of shape

Daily news

Children write, draw or fix photographs on small pieces of paper about any event that has happened that day. They place the pieces of paper onto A4 paper and arrange them until they are happy with the position, then glue or tape the pieces into place. With your help, they use a computer to print the date and use a flatbed scanner to scan the A4 paper. Children then distribute copies of the news to everyone.

Things to ask

Can you tell me about your arrangement of news?

Whereabouts did you decide to put the photographs?

Which shape did you choose to do your drawing on?

Look, listen, note

Which children can

- sequence the events of the day?
- identify the position of different shapes?
- arrange their news items on a piece of paper?

Challenge

Children work in pairs to make a double-spread newspaper.

Children keep a daily-news diary, using a large calendar.

Magic house

The magic house develops from the more traditional home corner. A book shared or a letter sent from a story character can change the house into another residence. The maths opportunities occur as furniture and resources are adapted to suit the new owners. Every time there are new residents and the magic house changes from, for example, the Three Bears' House to the Giant's Castle, the contents could be sorted, measured, counted and catalogued by the children. All the activities and games in this section are linked to traditional tales.

Maths learning chart

Maths content

Activities	Page	Number	Calculating	Shape and space	Measures	Problem solving
Red Riding Hood's journey	36	✿				✿
Rehousing the Three Little Pigs	37	✿				✿
Jack's beans	38		✿			✿
The shoemaker's card game	39		✿			✿
Gingerbread people	40	✿		✿		✿
Furnishing Bear's house	41			✿	✿	✿

Problem solving identified

Activities

Problem solving	Red Riding Hood's journey	Rehousing the Three Little Pigs	Jack's beans	The shoemaker's card game	Gingerbread people	Furnishing Bear's house
Solving problems		✿		✿	✿	✿
Representing	✿					
Decision making	✿	✿	✿	✿	✿	
Reasoning				✿		✿
Communicating		✿	✿	✿		

Making the most of your magic house

Resourcing the magic house

Encourage the group to help collect resources for the magic house: a wide range of furniture; crockery, cutlery, saucepans, kettle, tea sets, teapot; telephones, cooker, fridge, cupboards, sink, washing machine; dressing-up clothes, hats, fabric; shopping bags; dolls in various sizes, dolls clothes; clock; food, empty containers, cookery book; full-length mirror, magazines, bed, cot; iron and ironing board, broom; pushchair; books.

Developing a learning conversation

I wonder how we can find out the telephone number for the doctor?

Can you find some clothes to fit a baby?

How can we check if there are enough knives and forks for everyone?

Using ICT to support maths

Mobile phones

Digital camera

Maths toolkit

Number cards, number lines, measuring tapes, weighing balances and scales

Songs to sing

Jelly on a plate

Teddy bear, teddy bear

Miss Polly had a dolly

Books to read

Peace at Last by Jill Murphy (Picturemac)

The Tiger who Came to Tea by Judith Kerr (Picture Lions)

Once upon a Time by John Prater (Walker Books)

Don't Put Your Finger in the Jelly, Nelly! by Nick Sharratt (Scholastic)

Music to listen to

Children's overture by Roger Quilter

The Firebird by Igor Stravinsky

Red Riding Hood's journey

Children roll the dice, say the number and count along an unnumbered track from Red Riding Hood's house through the woods to her Granny's house. Children first construct the game board, using 20 blank squares for the path and trees from small-world materials to make the wood, and put a 'house' either end of the path. Children all choose a Red Riding Hood figure to move along the track to deliver food to Granny and return home.

You need

- 1–6 spotty dice
- 20 blank squares
- Trees to make a wood
- Two small boxes to be houses
- Play people as a Red Riding Hood figure for each child
- Pretend items to deliver to Granny

Things to ask

How many steps have you counted along the path?

What number do you need to roll to get exactly to Granny's house?

I wonder what will happen if you roll a 5?

Look, listen, note

Which children can

- recognise the dice patterns without counting?
- count accurately along the path?
- estimate the number of steps before they reach the house?

Challenge

Write some 'traps' along the path, such as 'See wolf, go back 2 steps'.

Children play the game again, taking other items to Granny.

Words to use

one, two, three ... six, count, how many?, number, dice pattern

Maths learning

Number

Using some number names

Counting along a track

Recognising dice patterns

Rehousing the Three Little Pigs

Children use 10 small recycled boxes to make a row of houses for the Three Little Pigs and their families. They choose a number card and make a house with that door number. They write labels to say which pig lives in which house, and they write the number on the front door of each house. Children put a pig in each house and arrange the houses in door number order.

You need

- 10 small recycled boxes such as cereal or teabag boxes
- A selection of materials to cover the outside of the boxes, such as straw, wrapping paper, small sticks
- Scissors
- Felt-tip pens
- 1–10 number cards
- Sticky labels
- Sticky coloured paper
- A number line for reference
- 10 small pigs

Things to ask

What can we do to remember the order the houses go in?

What numbers did you write on your front doors?

I wonder what house will go next to house number 4?

Look, listen, note

Which children can

- say the numbers to 10 in order?
- recognise what number to write on the door?
- use words such as 'first' and 'last' when discussing the order of the boxes?

Challenge

Children collect the door numbers that other children live in and look for them on a number line.

Children give each pig family a telephone number.

Words to use

one, two, three ... ten, next to, before, after, count, first, second, last

Maths learning

Number

Saying and using number names in order

Recognising numerals 1 to 9

Using ordinal numbers

Jack's beans

Children play in pairs. They decide who will be Red and who White. Children tip 10 coloured beans from a cup and count and compare how many beans land on red side up and how many land on white side up. The child with most beans landing their colour up wins a counter. If they have the same number of colour-up beans, both children win a counter. Children keep tossing and deciding whose colour has most until one child has won 10 counters.

You will need

- 10 dried butter beans, spray-painted red on one side, for each pair
- A plastic cup
- 20 counters for each pair
- A number track for reference

Things to ask

How did you decide who has most beans colour side up?

How many beans are there altogether?

Does it matter whether you choose red or white?

Look, listen, note

Which children can

- count the beans accurately?
- explain a strategy for deciding which colour has most?
- use the language of comparison?

Challenge

Children record the number pairs they roll.

Children find as many different number pairs as possible.

Words to use

one, two, three … ten, most, more, less, fewer, altogether

Maths learning

Calculating

Comparing two groups of objects

Using language such as 'more' or 'less' to compare two numbers

Counting to 10 objects

The shoemaker's card game

Children play a game with cards that have foot outlines arranged to represent dice number patterns (suggest that they make the cards themselves, using stickers). They share the shuffled cards between them and put them in two piles in front of them. They each turn over the card from the top of the pile. The child with the highest number takes both cards. Children keep playing until one child has got rid of all their cards. They are the winner.

Things to ask

What did you think was the best way to share out the cards?

How did you decide who had the most shoes on their cards?

What did you do when you both had the same number?

Look, listen, note

Which children can

- recognise the foot patterns?
- explain a strategy for deciding which card has the most?
- use the language of comparison?

Challenge

Children play the game so that the player with the lowest card takes both cards.

Children play the game again, using two packs of 1–10 number cards.

Words to use

one, two, three … six, more, most, less, fewer, same

Maths learning

Calculating

Comparing two groups of objects

Using language such as 'more' or 'less' to compare two numbers

Counting to 10 objects

Gingerbread people

Children decorate made or shop-bought gingerbread men with coloured icing and small sweets. They place the gingerbread men on greaseproof paper and add buttons and eyes. Children then measure and cut up rice paper to make a hat and trousers for their gingerbread men, using the plastic shapes as a guide for their patterns. They glue on the paper clothes, using icing from the tubes.

You need

- A gingerbread man for each child
- Tubes of different-coloured icing
- A selection of small sweets as buttons and eyes
- Greaseproof paper
- Sheets of rice paper to make clothes for the gingerbread men
- Scissors, glue
- Plastic shapes
- Measuring tapes

Things to ask

How many buttons do you need for your gingerbread man?

What shape will you choose for your gingerbread man's hat?

How did you know what size to make your gingerbread man's trousers?

Look, listen, note

Which children can

- count the sweets they need accurately?
- name the shapes they are using?
- use the language of measurement?

Challenge

Children weigh the ingredients and bake their own gingerbread men.

Children make a paper bag to carry their gingerbread man in.

Words to use

one, two, three, pair, how many?, more, less, size, shape, square, rectangle, circle, triangle, small, long, longer, short, shorter, big, bigger

Maths learning

Number and shape and space

Saying and using number names

Measuring and comparing sizes

Selecting named shapes

Furnishing Bear's house

Children cut out furniture and equipment pictures from magazines and catalogues. They divide a large piece of paper into 'rooms' and label them. They sort the cut-out pictures into the appropriate spaces and glue them on.

You will need

- A supply of magazines and catalogues
- Scissors
- A3 paper for each pair
- Glue
- Sticky labels

Things to ask

I wonder why you have put all those pictures together?

Which areas in Bear's house did you furnish?

Where did you decide to put Baby Bear's chair?

Look, listen, note

Which children can

- identify appropriate furniture for each room?
- sort pictures into different-sized sets?
- explain how they have sorted the pictures?

Challenge

Children sort the equipment in the home corner into different sizes.

Children make a furniture catalogue for Bear and his family.

Words to use

same, different, large, medium, small, big, bigger, biggest

Maths learning

Shape and space and measures

Categorising objects according to size

Sorting objects identifying similarities and differences

Presenting results using pictures

Library

Successful classroom libraries have different systems for categorising the books: for example, books about animals, books by the same author, large books, counting books. Involving children in sorting the books is a way of using books to support maths learning. Expanding library resources into story sacks and board games based on stories provides further opportunities for sorting, data handling and problem solving.

Maths learning chart

Maths content

Activities	Page	Number	Calculating	Shape and space	Measures	Problem solving
Book titles	44	✽				✽
Moving books	45	✽				✽
Book money	46		✽			✽
Vote for us	47		✽			✽
The big search	48	✽		✽		✽
Making bookmarks	49			✽	✽	✽

Problem solving identified

Activities

Problem solving	Book titles	Moving books	Book money	Vote for us	The big search	Making bookmarks
Solving problems		✽			✽	✽
Representing	✽		✽			
Decision making	✽		✽	✽	✽	✽
Reasoning				✽		
Communicating	✽	✽		✽	✽	

Making the most of your library

Resourcing the library

Encourage the group to help collect resources for the library: a wide range of storybooks, picture books, poetry and nursery rhyme books, information packs, big books; story sacks, puppet and magnetic props; storyteller chairs, story tent, cushions, beanbags, chairs and rugs; rhyme games, lotto games, board games linked to stories; alphabet frieze, alphabet lines; core books, book baskets labelled on low shelves; photograph books, comics, magazines, songs and music books, dual-language books.

Developing a learning conversation

Can you recite your favourite nursery rhyme?

What is the best way to sort the books?

Which five props did you collect to make a story box?

Using ICT to support maths

Computer data package for children to keep a record of the books they read

Tape recorder and headphones to record children's favourite number rhyme

Torches to help look at books in the story tent

Maths toolkit

Number cards, number line, clock, calendar, counting bricks, diary

Books to read

Charlie Cook's Favourite Book by Julia Donaldson and Axel Scheffler (Macmillan)

Library Lion by Michelle Knudsen (Walker Books)

Lulu Loves the Library by Anna McQuinn (Alana Books)

Delilah Darling is in the Library by Jeanne Willis (Puffin)

Songs to sing

Five little men in a flying saucer flew round the world one day

Five little monkeys jumping on the bed

Five little speckled frogs

Music to listen to

Gabriel's Oboe from *The Mission* soundtrack by Ennio Morricone

Piano Sonata No 16 in C Major by Wolfgang Amadeus Mozart

Book titles

Children arrange the front covers on the drawn track spaces, putting several covers on each space and leaving some spaces empty. They put their character on an empty space and take it in turns to roll the dice, say the number and move their small-world character that many spaces. Children choose a book cover from the space their character lands on. They keep going round the track until they have 'won' three books. They match the front covers to the actual books and read them.

Things to ask

How many spaces round the track do you need to move?

What number did you roll on the dice?

How will you know what space to take your book title from?

Look, listen, note

Which children can

- identify the numbers on the dice?
- say the numbers in the right order?
- count the moves round the track successfully?

Challenge

Children use book titles written on cards instead of front covers.

Children play the game again with a different collection of books.

Moving books

Children choose some number books to move from the shelf to an empty book basket. They roll the dice to move along a path of 10 carpet squares laid between the bookshelf and the basket. Children work in pairs. Child A rolls the dice and says the number; Child B holds the book and jumps that many spaces along the number track. When they reach the book basket, they turn round and jump back to the bookshelf. Children swap roles to take the next book to the basket.

You need

- A selection of number books
- A book basket
- 10 blank carpet tiles
- A 1–3 dice

Things to ask

How many jumps until you get to the end of the path?

Which counting book did you choose?

How many more books are you going to move?

Look, listen, note

Which children can

- explain how many jumps they need?
- count the number of books in the collection?
- use number names when asked how to explain playing the game?

Challenge

Extend the track to 20 and suggest children use a 1–6 dice.

Children make a list of the books they moved.

Words to use

one, two, three, how many?, count, jump, number track

Maths learning

Number

Counting actions

Saying and using number names in order

Counting to 10 objects

Book money

Children put a sticky note on each book and write a price from 1p to 5p on the note. They each have five 1p coins and take it in turns to roll the dice and move their counter that many spaces along the track. Where the counter lands, they 'give' or 'take' a penny from the money box. When they reach the end of the track, they count the pennies they have collected and buy the books they want to read.

Things to ask

How did you find out how much money you had collected?

How did you decide to split up your pennies?

Which book cost you the most?

Look, listen, note

Which children can

- find the total amount of pennies they have?
- divide their pennies to make different amounts?
- say which book cost the most?

Challenge

Children use 2p coins as well as 1p coins.

Children increase the cost of the books.

Vote for us

Children put together a collection of storybooks and discuss what they like about them. They take a sticker and put it on the card next to their favourite book. Children then count the star stickers and decide which book was everybody's most favourite.

Things to ask

How can we find out which book has the most star stickers?

Do you think there are more than five stickers on that book?

Does this book have more stars than that book?

Look, listen, note

Which children can

- say which book has the most or fewest stars?
- count the stars to find the total?
- use the language of comparison during discussion?

Challenge

Children make a graph to show the results of the vote.

Children choose another selection of books and vote on those.

The big search

In twos or threes, children read a counting book and choose a number from it. One of the group hides that number of small bears in the library area and then gives clues where the bears are hidden. The others search until they have found all the hidden bears. Children explain to each other where they found or hid each bear, then swap roles to play the game again

You need

- 20 small plastic counting bears
- A counting book

Things to ask

How many bears do you need to find?

Where was the first place you decided to look?

Did anyone find a bear next to the pencil pot?

Look, listen, note

Which children can

- describe where they found a bear?
- suggest places that the bears might be hidden?
- count how many bears they have found?

Challenge

Children draw a diagram to show where the objects were found.

Children find 10 more places to hide the bears.

Words to use

one, two, three ... ten, how many?, count, in, under, on top of, in front of, behind, next to, beside

Maths learning

Number and shape and space

Counting to 10 everyday objects

Using everyday words to describe position

Finding items from positional clues

Making bookmarks

Each child cuts a bookmark-shaped piece of recycled birthday card by drawing and cutting along two diagonal lines from one corner of the card to the other. Children then choose from a collection of metallic shape stickers to create a pattern on the blank side of the cut-out bookmark. Show the children how to punch a hole at the end of the bookmark and thread through a small bead on a string.

You need

- Recycled birthday cards
- Scissors
- Metallic shape stickers
- Hole punch
- Beads
- String
- Ruler

Things to ask

Do you think your bookmark will look best with straight or curved edges?

Can you describe the pattern you have made?

Can you describe the shapes you have left over?

Look, listen, note

Which children can

- name some of the shapes?
- talk about curved and straight lines?
- put the shapes together to create a pattern?

Challenge

Children make a bookmark for a friend, creating a different pattern.

Children draw 'How to make a bookmark' picture instructions on a large bookmark.

Words to use

shape, pattern, straight line, stars, circle, square, rectangle, curved lines

Maths learning

Shape and space and measures

Making arrangements of shapes

Using the language of shape

Talking about patterns and shapes

Explorer's workshop

The explorer's workshop is an area where the children can investigate, discover and extend their interest in the world around them. They have opportunities to experiment and find out how things work, take things apart and put them together again. Collections the children have gathered in the outdoor area can be brought back to the explorer's workshop to be investigated further. You can set up plenty of problem-solving scenarios in this workshop.

Maths learning chart

Activities	Page	Number	Calculating	Shape and space	Measures	Problem solving
Pizza picture boxes	52	❀				❀
Car construction	53	❀			❀	❀
Fridge magnet designs	54		❀			❀
Peg lines	55		❀			❀
Lid rescue	56			❀		❀
Serving pasta	57	❀			❀	❀

Problem solving identified

Problem solving	Pizza picture boxes	Car construction	Fridge magnet designs	Peg lines	Lid rescue	Serving pasta
Solving problems	❀	❀	❀		❀	❀
Representing	❀	❀	❀		❀	
Decision making	❀	❀	❀	❀		
Reasoning				❀		❀
Communicating	❀	❀		❀	❀	❀

Making the most of your explorer's workshop

Resourcing the workshop

Encourage the group to help collect resources for the explorer's workshop: natural materials such as conkers, fir cones, stones, gourds, dried flowers, shells; mirrors, light box, kaleidoscopes; living things such as plants, minibeasts, fish; magnets, colour filters, binoculars; fabrics, tactile materials; locks and keys; collections of things to touch, smell, taste.

Developing a learning conversation

How much jelly do you think you can fit in a jam jar?

How can we find out how many seeds are in a pumpkin?

Suppose you were making a house for a woodlouse. What would you do first?

Using ICT to support maths

Digital microscope to look closely at an object

Digital camera to photograph a favourite object

Overhead projector to observe the outline shape of an object

Light box to look at small details

Maths toolkit

Number cards, number lines, calculator, balances and scales, plastic counting cubes, tape measures

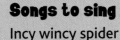

Songs to sing

Incy wincy spider

Books to read

The Tin Soldier by H C Andersen (a traditional tale)

Billy's Bucket by Kes Gray and Garry Parsons (Red Fox)

Sharing a Shell by Julia Donaldson and Lydia Monks (Macmillan)

Pumpkin Soup by Helen Cooper (Corgi)

Brown Bear, Brown Bear, What Do You See? by Bill Martin and Eric Carle (Picture Puffin)

Music to listen to

Hebrides Overture (Fingal's Cave Overture) by Felix Mendelssohn

Rodeo by Aaron Copland

Pizza picture boxes

Children use pizza delivery boxes as 3D picture frames to make a picture number line. They choose a number less than 6 and write it on the lid of the box. Children then open the box, line it and glue on a range of collage materials in groups that reflect the number written on the box lid. When the boxes are complete, children arrange them in number order.

Things to ask

Are you making a picture box for more or less than 3?

How will you know how many sequins to stick into your box?

I wonder what number is written on the front of this box?

Look, listen, note

Which children can

- recognise and say some number names?
- count out the collage materials they are using?
- read the appropriate numeral on other boxes?

Challenge

Children make boxes to 10.

Children arrange the boxes into a number line and display them on the wall.

Words to use

zero, one, two, three, four, how many?, count, numeral

Maths learning

Number

Using some number names

Counting reliably to five objects

Recognising numerals to 5

Car construction

With the children, discuss using recycled materials to build cars for play people to ride in. Discuss how many wheels each car will need and how many passengers it will hold. Support the children in constructing the cars and talk about and estimate how far the cars might travel. Together, make a ramp and record how many play people are in each car and how far the car travelled from the ramp.

You need

- Various small wheels
- Construction materials
- Small-world people as passengers
- A ramp or slope for the cars to run down
- Length-measuring materials such as metre sticks, ribbon, string

Things to ask

How many will ride in the car?

How far will it travel?

What can you use to measure the distance your car travelled?

Look, listen, note

Which children can

- decide how to measure the distance?
- use appropriate numbers when referring to their measures?
- count accurately?

Challenge

Children make a large car from boxes that a child can sit in.

Children use a wind-up toy car and measure how far it can travel.

Words to use

how far?, how many?, more, less, furthest, nearest, start from

Maths learning

Number and measures

Using some number names

Recognising groups with one, two or three objects

Counting out a specified number from a larger group

Fridge magnet designs

In pairs, children choose from a collection of fridge magnets to make a picture or pattern arrangement on a baking tray. They take it in turns to pick two digit cards and choose that many magnets to make their picture.

Things to ask

How many magnets did you choose?

I wonder how you know that you find out the total number of magnets?

Can you tell me about your picture?

Look, listen, note

Which children can

- choose the right number of magnets?
- talk about the picture they have made?
- count out the magnets from the collection?

Challenge

Children take a number card and swap that number of magnets with another pair.

Children write a label to go with their picture, explaining how many magnets they used and the story of the picture.

Words to use

one, two, three … ten, how many?, count, more, fewer, total, altogether

Maths learning

Calculating

Making arrangements with objects

Counting out objects from a larger group

Noticing patterns in pictures

Peg lines

Children choose two digit cards. They say the numbers, add them together and pick up that many pegs. They peg the pegs onto a washing line. In the next round, they choose one card and take away that many pegs from the washing line. When they have 10 pegs on their line, children choose some scarves to peg up and display.

Things to ask

How many pegs have you got altogether?

I wonder how many pegs there will be when you take two away?

How many scarves will you be able to hang up with your pegs?

Look, listen, note

Can the children

- count out the pegs accurately?
- find the total number of pegs by counting?
- explain how to work out how many scarves they can peg up?

Challenge

Children find out how many pegs they need to peg up 10 scarves.

Children arrange and count the pegs in twos.

Words to use

one, two, three ... ten, altogether, total, how many?, add, take away

Maths learning

Calculating

Counting reliably to 10 everyday objects

Finding the total number of objects in two groups by counting

Using the vocabulary involved in adding and taking away

Lid rescue

Put out a large collection of different containers with lids. Children examine all the containers, remove the lids and put them in a pillowcase. They take it in turns to remove a lid. If they can put it on the right container, they have 'won' it. Children continue to choose lids until all the containers have a lid.

You need

- About 12 containers with lids, such as plastic jars, bottles, saucepans, teapots and tins in different shapes and sizes
- Pillowcase

Things to ask

Can you say why you think that lid will fit the teapot?

I wonder why that lid doesn't fit the bottle?

Does anyone know what shape lid would fit this jar?

Look, listen, note

Which children can

- explain why they have chosen a particular lid?
- use the language of shape in discussion?
- suggest two containers that have similar properties?

Challenge

Children draw round the containers lids.

Children record the containers everyone collected.

Words to use

shape, size, circle, square, rectangle, hexagon, too small, too large, similar, same, different

Maths learning

Shape and space

Discussing shapes of everyday objects

Using the language of shape

Identifying similarities and differences

Serving pasta

Fill a shallow water tray half full with cooked spaghetti and cover with water. Provide different types of tongs for children to use to fill small containers with the pasta.

You need

- Packets of long spaghetti
- A selection of different-sized tongs such as teabag holders, spaghetti tongs
- Pasta serving spoons
- Shallow water tray and water
- Plastic bowls of various sizes

Things to ask

How will you know when your bowl is full up with spaghetti?

I wonder which is the longest piece of spaghetti you can find?

How many pieces of spaghetti do you think you can pick up?

Look, listen, note

Which children can

- describe when the container is full?
- find a short piece of spaghetti and point out a longer piece?
- count lengths of spaghetti using one number name for each object?

Challenge

Children use spaghetti to half fill different-sized bowls.

Children put some strands of spaghetti in order of length.

Words to use

full, half full, empty, how many?, one, two three ... ten, long, thin, short

Maths learning

Number and measures

Filling and emptying containers

Describing different lengths

Counting objects

Horticulture

Young children just love gardening, and even the most humble digging patch offers great opportunities for discovering worms and developing maths ideas. Make sure that there are resources available when children need to measure the height of the sunflowers and to think about how far apart to plant the bulbs or the straight line that the lettuces need to be set in. A garden area has great potential for data-handling activities: all the beetles, ants and ladybirds need to be counted, tomatoes and beans need to be harvested and weighed …

Maths learning chart

Maths content

Activities	Page	Number	Calculating	Shape and space	Measures	Problem solving
The seed game	60	✿				✿
Surveying minibeasts	61	✿				✿
Sowing sunflowers	62		✿			✿
Sorting everything	63	✿	✿			✿
The potato-picking game	64	✿			✿	✿
Pairing up wellies	65		✿		✿	✿

Problem solving identified

Activities

Problem solving	The seed game	Surveying minibeasts	Sowing sunflowers	Sorting everything	The potato-picking game	Pairing up wellies
Solving problems		✿				✿
Representing	✿				✿	
Decision making			✿			
Reasoning				✿		✿
Communicating		✿				

Making the most of your garden centre

Resourcing the garden centre

Encourage the group to help collect resources for the garden centre: old logs, stones for minibeasts, rocks; digging patch or compost tray, growing bags, pots in various sizes, seeds; garden tools, buckets, wheelbarrows, closed-top water butt; wormery; collecting pots, pooters, magnifying glasses, clipboards with pencils attached; wellies.

Developing a learning conversation

How could we find out how many minibeasts live on the tomato plant?

Can you tell us what is the same about those two wellies and what is different?

Can you guess how many cherries you can hold in one hand?

Using ICT to support maths

Digital camera

Electronic measure

Digital microscope and laptop

Maths toolkit

Measuring tape, metre sticks, balance scales, number lines, string and pegs

Songs to sing

There's a worm at the bottom of the garden

Hedgehog is very prickly

Dingle dangle scarecrow

Mary, Mary, quite contrary

Music to listen to

The Lark Ascending by Ralph Vaughan Williams

The Flight of the Bumblebee by Nikolai Rimsky-Korsakov

Books to read

The Little Mouse, the Red Ripe Strawberry and the Big Hungry Bear by Don and Audrey Wood (Childs Play)

The Very Busy Spider by Eric Carle (Grosset & Dunlap)

Billy's Beetle by Mick Inkpen (Hodder Children's Book)

Billy's Sunflower by Nicola Moon (Scholastic Little Hippo)

Wibbly's Garden by Mick Inkpen (Hodder Children's Books)

Ten Seeds by Ruth Brown (Andersen Press)

In addition: seed catalogues, gardening books and magazines

The seed game

Give each child in the group the top of an aerosol can to use as a plant pot. Put a box of pumpkin seeds in the middle of the table. Children take it in turns to toss the dice, take that many seeds from the box and put them in their plant pot. After everyone has had three throws of the dice, they count all the seeds in their pot and compare how many seeds they each have collected.

Things to ask

What number patterns do you recognise on the dice?

Can you explain how to play the game?

How can you find out how many seeds you collected in your pot?

Look, listen, note

Which children can

- count out the seeds accurately?
- explain how to play the game?
- recognise the numerals on the dice?

Challenge

Children write a number card to go alongside their pot.

Children count 10 seeds into their pots, roll the dice and take that many seeds out of their pot.

Words to use

number, one, two, three … ten, add, how many?, how many altogether?, collect, count

Maths learning

Number

Counting reliably to 10 everyday objects

Using language to compare two quantities

Counting out from a larger group

Surveying minibeasts

Ask the children to record the minibeasts they see while they are digging in the garden. Discuss what they are likely to see based on their previous observations. Using collecting pots and magnifying glasses, children study the minibeasts before carefully releasing them again.

You need
- Collecting pots
- Magnifying glasses
- Clipboards and pencils

Things to ask

How many worms, woodlice, millipedes did you see?

Which minibeast did you see the most?

Can you think of a way of recording how many you saw?

Look, listen, note

Which children can

- talk about the activity when it is completed?
- suggest ways of recording their observations?
- count and compare the number of minibeasts in each category?

Challenge

Children choose one kind of minibeast and see how many they can find.

Extend the survey for a week and discuss the data collected.

Words to use

how many?, count, zero, none, same different, one, two, three … ten

Maths learning

Number

Counting reliably to 10 everyday objects

Developing mathematical ideas and methods to solve practical problems

Using language to compare quantities

Sowing sunflowers

Give each child two pots, a trowel or large spoon and a stick or dibber. Children use the trowel to fill up their flower pots with compost. Together with the children, decide to which level the compost needs to come up to for a full pot. Ask the group to estimate the number of trowelfuls they need to fill the pot. Show the children how to press a small stick or dibber into the compost to plant a seed. Talk about how many seeds to put in the pot. Children then count out how many seeds they need altogether. They write a label to show how many seeds are planted in the pot.

You need

• Plastic plant pots
• Trowels or spoons
• Small sticks or dibbers
• Compost
• Sunflower seeds
• Labels

Things to ask

How many seeds do you need altogether?

I wonder how many seed holes you have made?

How will you know if there is enough compost in your pot?

Look, listen, note

Which children can

• count out the seeds accurately?
• count the total number of seeds they have planted?
• explain how to work out how many seed holes they needed to make?

Challenge

Children find out how many trowels of compost they need to fill five pots.

Children draw an instruction poster on how to plant seeds.

Words to use

full, empty, half full, one, two, three … ten, how many?, altogether

Maths learning

Calculating

Counting reliably to 10 everyday objects

Finding the total number of items in two groups by counting

Using the vocabulary involved in adding

Sorting everything

Together, children make a collection of natural objects in the garden, such as twigs, conkers, leaves, seeds and petals. They roll the dice, say the number and pick up that many objects from the collection. Children then sort them into their own small boxes that are labelled 1 to 6. They can put the objects into one box or share them among all their boxes. The game is over when everybody has got the right number of things in each box.

You need

- A collection of natural objects
- A 1–6 dice
- A selection of small boxes labelled 1 to 6 for each child

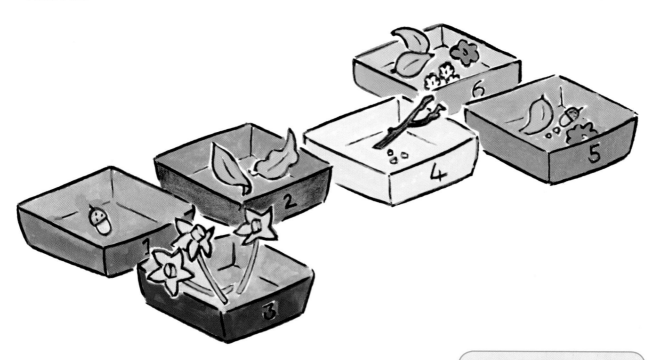

Things to ask

How many more objects do you need in your '6' box?

How will you share out the conkers?

Which box has the most objects?

Look, listen, note

Which children can

- count how many objects are in each box?
- suggest which box has most objects?
- explain how to share objects between the boxes?

Challenge

Children only put the same type of object in each box.

Children start with full boxes and take out objects.

Words to use

one, two, three … ten, more, less, altogether, total, fewer, same, one more, one less

Maths learning

Number and calculating

Counting to 10 objects

Using the language of comparison

Share objects into groups

The potato-picking game

Children throw the dice, say the number and use a pair of tongs to pick up that many potatoes from a box of compost. They put the picked potatoes into their vegetable boxes. Children keep taking turns until all the potatoes have been picked. They then line up their potatoes to see who can make the longest line of picked potatoes, using measuring tape or a piece of string.

You need

- One 1–3 dice
- A pair of cooking tongs
- 500 g of small new potatoes (about 25 potatoes)
- A shallow box or tray filled with compost to bury the potatoes in
- A small plastic vegetable box for each child
- Measuring tapes or string

Things to ask

How did you know how many potatoes to pick?

How can we line up the potatoes to compare them?

Can you guess whose box of potatoes is going to make the longest line?

Look, listen, note

Which children can

- pick up the number of potatoes shown on the dice?
- suggest ways of measuring the potato lines?
- compare the lines of potatoes and identify the longest?

Challenge

Children use a 1–6 dice and more potatoes.

Children cook the picked potatoes and eat them.

Words to use

one, two, three, how many?, long, longer, longest, short, shorter, shortest, count, measure

Maths learning

Number and measures

Saying and using number names in order

Using the vocabulary of length

Ordering three items by length

Pairing up wellies

On a rainy day, suggest to the children that they pair up wellies to make sure that they are all there and none are missing. After that, they go outside and do a welly raindance.

Things to ask

I wonder how we can start sorting out the wellies?

How will we know when two wellies are a pair?

Is your welly longer or shorter than this one?

Look, listen, note

Which children can

- suggest how to start sorting the wellies?
- offer ideas on why two particular wellies are a pair?
- use measurement words when describing the size of the wellies?

Challenge

Children put some of the pairs in order of size.

Children find a way of labelling each pair of wellies.

Words to use

pairs, in twos, odd, even, count, pattern, same as, different, sort, big, bigger, biggest, small, smaller, smallest

Maths learning

Calculating and measures

Using mathematical ideas and methods to solve practical problems

Using language of size

Sorting familiar objects and justifying decisions

Theatre

A theatre workshop is an exciting stage for creative play. Dressing-up fantasy and pretend play are just magic and give all children a scenario for developing maths skills and understanding maths. Using a wooden patio area or stage blocks as a theatre provides opportunities for lots of problem solving as children measure and paint scenery backdrops, count steps for a dance routine, put together outfits and decide what costumes to wear.

Maths learning chart

Maths content

Activities	Page	Number	Calculating	Shape and space	Measures	Problem solving
Musical instruments	68	✿				✿
Number dance	69	✿				✿
The accessory game	70		✿			✿
Superheroes dressing-up game	71		✿			✿
Scenery makers	72				✿	✿
Spectacle masks	73			✿	✿	✿

Problem solving identified

Activities

Problem solving	Musical struments	Number dance	The accessory game	Superheroes dressing-up game	Scenery makers	Spectacle masks
Solving problems			✿		✿	✿
Representing	✿	✿				
Decision making		✿	✿	✿		✿
Reasoning				✿	✿	
Communicating	✿		✿			

Resourcing the theatre

Encourage the group to help collect resources for the theatre: a range of musical instruments; a variety of fabrics and dressing-up clothes, stage make-up and paints; puppet and story props; large sheets of paper, large rollers, pots of paint.

Developing a learning conversation

How can we decide how many people can watch the show?

Does anyone know a way to find out how wide the curtains need to be?

What would you suggest that the ticket price should be?

Using ICT to support maths

Video to record the rehearsals and the show

Microphone for singing

Cash register to collect the ticket money

Maths toolkit

Money, calculator, number cards, large number square, grid paper

Songs to sing

When Goldilocks went to the house of the bears

There was a princess long ago

Books to read

When I Grow Up by Colin McNaughton (Walker Books)

Harry's Box by Angela McAllister (Bloomsbury Paperbacks)

Angelina Ballerina by Helen Craig and Katherine Holabird (Pheasant Company Publications)

Music to listen to

Entry of the Gladiators by Julius Fucik

Swan Lake – Pas de Quatre Small Swans by Piotr Tchaikovsky

Another Opening, Another Show by Cole Porter

Musical instruments

Everyone in the group chooses a musical instrument. After a short practice session with their instrument, children take it in turns to choose a number card and play their instrument that many times. Everyone else guesses what number was written on the card.

Things to ask

How many beats did you play?

Who thinks they heard more than three beats?

I wonder how many beats you would play if you had this number card?

Look, listen, note

Which children can

- read the numbers on the card?
- count the beats they are making?
- explain how they knew how many beats they heard?

Challenge

Children choose two number cards at each turn.

Children make music using a repeating number pattern such as 1, 2, 1, 2.

Words to use
one, two three ...
nine, count, how

Maths learning
Number
Matching number and quantity
Counting actions to 9
Recognising numerals 1 to 9

Number dance

Arrange numbered carpet tiles in a circle (alternatively, use hoops and pieces of paper with numbers written on). Children dance round the circle in time to the music. When the music stops, they jump onto a number square and write the number they are standing on in the air, using their ribbon.

You need

- Source of music
- 1–9 numbered carpet tiles or hoops with numbers in
- A length of ribbon attached to a stick or plastic straw for each child

Things to ask

What number are you standing on?

I wonder what number you are writing in the air?

Is anybody writing the number that is 'one more' than 5?

Look, listen, note

Which children can

- recognise the number they are standing on?
- write their number using the ribbons?
- tell the number that is 'one more' or 'one less' than the number they are standing on?

Challenge

Children play the game with the number tiles arranged in random order.

Children use the ribbons to air write any number, but not the number they are standing on.

Words to use

one, two three ... nine, start, stop, next number, last number, one more, one less

Maths learning

Number

Using number names

Representing numbers

Recognising numerals to 9

The accessory game

The group sorts the accessories into separate, labelled baskets. Children take it in turns to roll both dice and say the numbers. They then choose a selection of accessories that total the numbers on the dice. When they have shared out all the accessories, children count how many they have altogether and put them on. They announce their real name to the rest of the group and who they are pretending to be on the day.

Things to ask

How many have you got to collect altogether?

Do you have more or less than your friend?

Have you got the same number of anything?

Look, listen, note

Which children can

- work out how many items they need to collect?
- explain how they are counting their objects?
- explain the numbers they added?

Challenge

Children use a 1–6 dice.

Children try to remove their items by using a dice and subtraction.

Maths learning

Calculating

Knowing that the quantity changes when something is added or taken away

Making comparisons between quantities

Selecting two groups to make a given total of objects

Superheroes dressing-up game

Play the superheroes dressing-up game on the stage. Arrange the heroes' dressing-up clothes in a wicker box with a lid. Children take it in turns to take a card. They say the number, toss the 'one more'/'one less' counter and say the revised number. They open the box and choose that many items of clothing. Encourage the children to keep rolling the dice and tossing the counter until everyone is dressed up as a superhero. Have a parade of superheroes and a group and individual photocall.

You need

- A wicker box with a lid
- Superheroes' dressing-up clothes
- 1–5 number cards, shuffled
- Large counter labelled 'one more' on one side and 'one less' on the reverse
- Counters, cubes, number line to support calculation
- Stage blocks
- Camera

Things to ask

What number card did you pick up?

Do you think you will you have more or fewer clothes?

I wonder how we could find out how many pieces of dressing-up clothes you are wearing?

Look, listen, note

Which children can

- say the number that is 'one more'/'one less'?
- use language such as 'more' or 'less' to compare two numbers?
- use their own methods to work out calculation?

Challenge

Children print out individual photos and recreate the superheroes' parade for a class display.

Children swap some items of clothing with another superhero.

Words to use

one, two, three, more or fewer one more, one less, total, add, take away

Maths learning

Calculating

Finding 'one more' or 'one less'

Using the language of calculation

Making comparisons between quantities

Scenery makers

Set up a scenery-makers' guild of painters. Using different lengths of wallpaper laid out on a paste table, children roller on colour for a backdrop for dramatic play. Provide a range of colours and different-sized rollers for children to explore various effects.

Things to ask

Is the wallpaper long enough?

I wonder what we could use to measure the length?

What size roller will you choose?

Look, listen, note

Which children can

- decide which length of wallpaper is needed?
- talk about the different sizes they will use as a backdrop?
- sort the lengths of wallpaper into size order?

Challenge

Children measure and paint the backing for a display board.

Children use extra large rollers and paint a sheet to use as scenery.

Words to use

long, longer, longest, short, shorter, shortest, measure, size, length

Maths learning

Measures

Discussing variations in size

Using the language of length

Ordering items by length

Spectacle masks

Explain to the children that the theatre group needs some more masks for stage props. Say that the masks need not cover the mouth, because people in the audience want to hear what the actors and actresses are saying when they are on stage. Show the spectacles: talk about their shape and discuss different ways of decorating them.

You need

- A supply of children's toy plastic sunglasses, with glass removed
- Materials for decorating frames: curled ribbons, beads, sequins, feathers, and so on
- Glue

Things to ask

What materials are you going to choose?

Where will you glue your ribbons?

How long does your ribbon need to be?

Look, listen, note

Which children can

- tell what materials they have selected?
- identify how long their ribbons need to be?
- describe where they need to glue the decoration material?

Challenge

Children act out a drama, wearing the glasses they decorated.

Children mentor another child while they are decorating glasses.

Words to use

how long?, how much?, top, sides, underneath, how many?

Maths learning

Shape and space and measures

Describing different lengths

Talking about own choices and decisions

Using the language of position

Vehicle stop

Bikes, pushchairs, scooters, wheelbarrows, carts and all the other wheels make wonderful vehicles for some really good maths learning activities. The children can do a tally of how many wheels are in the area altogether and decide how to organise them so that there are fair shares. Let the children decide what vehicles to put out to make up that number: for example, they could have an 'only scooters' day or a maximum of 10 wheels in the area one day and less or more the next. Encourage the children to number every vehicle and to place it in its own numbered parking bay.

Maths learning chart

Maths content

Activities	Page	Number	Calculating	Shape and space	Measures	Problem solving
The toll gate	76	✿				✿
Cycling routes	77	✿				✿
Obstacle course	78		✿			✿
Key search	79		✿			✿
Shape deliveries	80			✿		✿
Wet-tyre printing	81				✿	✿

Problem solving identified

Activities

Problem solving	The toll gate	Cycling routes	Obstacle course	Key search	Shape deliveries	Wet-tyre printing
Solving problems			✿		✿	✿
Representing				✿		✿
Decision making		✿			✿	
Reasoning	✿			✿		
Communicating		✿				✿

Making the most of your vehicle stop

Resourcing the vehicle stop

Encourage the group to help collect resources for the vehicle stop: wheeled toys; prams, scooters, pushchairs, bikes, cooperative bikes, tricycles, trailers, balance bikes, wheelbarrows, pedal cars, tyres; maps, route directions; cones, road signs, torches, reflective clothing, zebra crossing; tool box, rescue vehicle, pulleys; parking bays; chalks.

Developing a learning conversation

How can you work out the shortest route round the outside area?

I wonder which bike is the most popular?

What vehicle do you think is best for transporting the bricks?

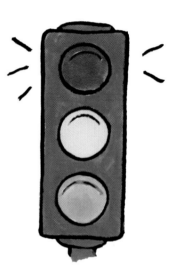

Using ICT to support maths

Walkie-talkies to communicate between vehicle riders

Mobile phones to call home

Stopwatch to time how fast you can go round the route

Maths toolkit

Stopwatches, sand timers, large laminated numbers, large dice, measuring tapes, metre sticks, number flip cards, number carpet tiles

Books to read

Wheels (Tales from Trotter Street) by Shirley Hughes (Walker Books)

The Big Concrete Lorry (Tales from Trotter Street) by Shirley Hughes (Walker Books)

Mr Gumpy's Motor Car by John Burningham (Harper Collins)

Percy's Bumpy Ride by Nick Butterworth (Collins)

Music to listen to

The Ride of the Valkyries by Richard Wagner

Carmina Burana by Carl Orff

Get Your Motor Running by Steppenwolf

Songs to sing

The wheels on the bus

Daisy, daisy

This is the way we wash the bikes

The big red bus

The toll gate

Put number labels on bikes and other wheeled vehicles and write matching numbers on parking spaces. Children take bikes by recording their name next to the relevant number on the bike grid. Make part of the cycle route a toll road where children 'pay' to cycle round. Establish a payment system where children pay 1p every time they pass the toll box. Make part of the cycle route a toll road where children 'pay' to cycle round it.

Things to ask

Can you say what number scooter you are riding?

How many pennies do you think are in the box?

How can we find out how many children rode past the toll gate?

Look, listen, note

Which children can

- identify the numbers on bikes or parking spaces?
- count the pennies correctly?
- use number names in discussion?

Challenge

Children make a tally chart for toll-gate users.

Introduce various toll-gate charges depending on the vehicle.

Words to use

one, two, three ... ten, count, number, penny, how much?, how many?, total

Maths learning

Number

Estimating how many coins there are

Counting everyday objects

Recognising numerals

Cycling routes

Chalk a circular cycling route on the ground. Children sort all the different numerals into same-numeral sets and put them in the appropriate labelled box. They place the boxes in order at intervals along the chalked route. Children write down the numbers 1 to 6 in any order on the route cards and then give it to another child to collect. As they cycle around the route, they collect the numerals in that order.

You need

- A circular chalked route
- Sets of 1 to 6 numerals in an assortment of materials such as wooden, plastic, printed cards
- Six boxes labelled 1 to 6
- Small rectangular pieces of card as route cards
- Pencils

Things to ask

What numeral have you got to collect first?

What can you say about the numerals in the third box?

Can you remember in what order you collected your numerals?

Look, listen, note

Which children can

- recognise the numerals on the box?
- use ordinal language while they are collecting?
- describe their route?

Challenge

Use a timer and have children complete one of the routes before the sand runs out.

Children use 1–10 number cards and put them into the right order at the end of the route.

Words to use

one, two, three ... six, first, second, third, last, next, before, after

Maths learning

Number

Recognising numerals to 6

Describing routes and position

Using ordinal number words

Obstacle course

Children set up an obstacle course, using cones and other objects to make a twisting roadway. In pairs, they pick a card with a number from 1 to 6 and choose a vehicle or combination of vehicles with that many wheels. Together, they ride or walk them round the obstacle course.

Things to ask

How many wheels do you need altogether to take round the obstacle?

I wonder if there are two vehicles where the wheels add up to 5?

If you include the scooter in your wheel count, will you have more wheels than you need or the right number?

Look, listen, note

Which children can

- suggest which vehicles to add that would give the wheel total they need?
- discuss the possible combinations there might be when adding vehicle wheel numbers?
- use a strategy to find the total number after adding more wheels?

Challenge

Groups of three children take up to 10 wheels round the obstacle course.

Children use a number line to work out all the possible combinations of vehicles for different wheel totals.

Words to use

one two, three, four, five, six, number, how many?, how many altogether?, total, more, less

Maths learning

Calculating

Knowing that a group of things changes when something is added

Finding the total number of items in two groups

Using the language of calculation

Key search

Children use a wheeled vehicle to look for and collect keys that have been hidden in the area. They keep a tally of how many of each colour they find and stop searching when they have collected six keys altogether.

You need

- A selection of wheeled vehicles, including bikes, prams, pushchairs, scooters and trucks
- A supply of keys tagged with either red or green ribbon
- Collecting bags
- Clipboards, pencils and tally sheets

Things to ask

Which colour key did you find the most of?

How did you know that your total was 6?

If you wanted to collect the same number of each colour, how many would that be?

Look, listen, note

Which children can

- identify which colour key was the most?
- explain a way of finding the total?
- use a strategy to work out equal numbers of the same colour?

Challenge

Children search for three different-coloured keys and add up the final total.

Children draw a map of where they found each key.

Words to use

one, two, three ... six, number, how many?, how many altogether?, total, more, less, same as

Maths learning

Calculating

Knowing that a group of things changes when something is added

Finding the total number of items in two groups

Using the language of calculation

Shape deliveries

Chalk pathways and shapes such as triangles, squares and circles on the ground. Children collect a parcel from the distribution table and look at the label to find out which shape it needs to be delivered to. They then choose a vehicle and pedal or push it round the drawn routes to deliver their parcel to the matching shape.

You need

- Wrapped parcels with a triangle-, square- or circle-shaped label on each
- A table
- A selection of wheeled vehicles, including bikes, prams, pushchairs, scooters and trucks
- Three large triangle, square, circle shapes chalked on the ground
- Chalked pathways that lead from the distribution table to a shape chalked on the ground

Things to ask

What shape parcel are you delivering?

How will you know which shape to deliver to?

Can you see that shape anywhere else?

Look, listen, note

Which children can

- match the parcel label to the shape drawn on the ground?
- talk about the shape parcel they are delivering and the route they are taking?
- identify a named shape such as a triangle or square?

Challenge

Extend the shape range to include hexagons and rectangles.

Children sort out a collection of shapes into different sets.

Words to use

shape, circle, square, triangle, straight lines, curved, corners

Maths learning

Shape and space

Matching shapes and recognising similarities

Using the language of shape

Selecting a particular named shape

Wet-tyre printing

Create a puddle by laying a plastic sheet on the ground and pouring on water that you have coloured with a small amount of paint. Put a length from a roll of wallpaper on one side of the puddle and invite children to ride through the puddle onto the paper to leave a wet-tyre mark. Put down fresh paper for each rider. With the children, measure the length of the tyre print, using string, ribbon, measuring tapes or ruler. Children compare the measurements from different riders.

You need

- A plastic sheet
- Water coloured with paint
- A roll of wallpaper cut into long lengths
- Bikes or scooters
- String or ribbon for measuring
- Measuring tapes or rulers

Things to ask

Which do you think is the longest tyre print?

Why do you know that is the shortest print?

Can anyone see a print longer than this one?

Look, listen, note

Which children can

- use words such as 'longer' or 'shorter' in discussion?
- say which is a longer length than an identified tyre print?
- put two or three print lengths in order?

Challenge

Children make a graph of print lengths.

Children display and label the prints.

Words to use

how long?, longer, longest, measure, start, end, measuring tape, ruler

Maths learning

Measures

Using the language of length

Comparing lengths

Ordering by length

Sports centre

A sports centre workshop supports children's developing climbing, balancing and throwing skills. A climbing frame makes a wonderful centrepiece for a sports centre, where, over time, you can add different pieces of equipment such as skipping ropes and hoops as an extension. Using the outdoor area for lots of running, jumping and hopping along huge number tracks, for example, is a good way to engage children in exploring maths learning on a large scale.

Maths learning chart

Maths content

Activities	Page	Number	Calculating	Shape and space	Measures	Problem solving
Pathway hop	84	✿				✿
Sorting out the balls	85	✿				✿
Ten-pin bowling	86		✿			✿
Goals	87		✿			
Circuit training	88			✿	✿	✿
Lifting weights	89				✿	✿

Problem solving identified

Activities

Problem solving	Pathway hop	Sorting out the balls	Ten-pin bowling	Goals	Circuit training	Lifting weights
Solving problems		✿	✿		✿	✿
Representing	✿		✿	✿	✿	
Decision making		✿				✿
Reasoning		✿				✿
Communicating	✿			✿		

Making the most of your sports centre

Resourcing the sports centre

Encourage the group to help collect resources for the sports centre: a range of different-sized balls, quoits, hoops, skittles skipping ropes; beanbags; climbing equipment, tunnels, benches, floor mats; bats, goal nets, parachutes, ladders.

Developing a learning conversation

I wonder if it is possible to make a square shape with a skipping rope?

What can we do to remember how many star jumps you can do?

Can you think of a way to make a walkway across the sports centre?

Using ICT to support maths

Video camera to create an action highlights film

Calculator programmed to be a repeating counter

Stopwatch to time how long it takes
to do pigeon steps from one area to the next

Maths toolkit

Stopwatches, sand timers, measuring tapes, number cards, score boards, magnetic board and numbers, number tracks and lines, interlocking cubes, white board and marker pen

Books to read

Cat Among the Cabbages by Alison Bartlett (Gullane Children's Books)

Hit the Ball, Duck by Jez Alborough (Harper Collins)

Goal! by Colin McNaughton (Harper Collins)

Songs to sing

Head, shoulders, knees and toes

One finger, one thumb, keep moving

Hokey cokey

If you're happy and you know it,
clap your hands

Music to listen to

Let's Get Started by the Black Eyed Peas

Brandenberg Concerto No 1 by Johann Sebastian Bach

We are the Champions by Queen

Pathway hop

Lay 15 unnumbered carpet tiles in a straight line to make a path. At the end of the path, position an easel with a recording grid. Children write their name on the grid. They take it in turns to throw the dice, say the number and hop that many squares along the path. Every time they reach the end of the path, they draw a tick by their name on the grid and start again on the path. The game is over when a child has drawn three ticks by their name.

Things to ask

How will you know how many squares to hop?

Is there a way we can find out who hopped the most?

How many ticks did you make next to your name?

Look, listen, note

Which children can

- recognise the numeral on the dice?
- make the right number of hops?
- read the recordings on the easel?

Challenge

Extend the path to 20 tiles. Reaching the end of the path, children turn back and hop to the start of the path.

Use numbered tiles for the path.

Words to use

one, two three ... six, count, number, how many?, forward, backward

Maths learning

Number

Using some number names

Counting actions

Recognising numbers to 6

Sorting out the balls

Resource the sports centre with a sack of different balls for children to sort. Children tip out the balls into a large box and decide how to sort them. This could be by colour (*These balls are all yellow*), by size (*These balls are all small*) or by usage (*These are all footballs*). Provide labels and hoops or boxes for sorted sets as well as number cards to indicate how many balls there are in the sorted sets.

You need

- A collection of different-sized balls
- A large box
- Hoops, boxes or buckets for the sorted balls
- Labels
- 1–10 number cards

Things to ask

What types of balls are there in the sack?

How will you sort the balls?

Which hoop do you think has got the most balls in?

Look, listen, note

Which children can

- explain their criteria for sorting?
- use counting to establish how many are in each set?
- match the appropriate number card to the set?

Challenge

Children re-sort the balls, using other criteria.

Children write property labels for each set.

Words to use

one, two, three … ten, count, how many?, the same, different, more, fewer

Maths learning

Number

Using number words and number language

Counting reliably

Matching sets of objects to numerals

Ten-pin bowling

Create a tunnel ramp by balancing one end of the tunnel on a low stool. Children arrange five skittles at the bottom of the ramp and take it in turns to roll a large ball through the tunnel in order to knock down as many skittles as possible. They keep a tally of how many skittles they knock over.

Things to ask

I wonder what is the best way to arrange the skittles?

Did you knock down more skittles with your first or second ball?

How will you work out how many skittles you knocked down altogether?

Look, listen, note

Which children can

- use a system for recording how many skittles they knocked down with each ball?
- find their total score by counting or adding?
- use the vocabulary of calculation?

Challenge

Children increase the number of skittles to 10.

Children use smaller balls.

Words to use

one, two, three … ten, how many?, count, more, fewer, one more, one less, score, total

Maths learning

Calculating

Knowing that the quantity changes when something is added

Finding the total number in two groups by counting

Using the vocabulary involved in adding

Goals

Set out a goal-scoring area with a goal and white tape or a chalk line about 3 to 5 metres from the goal. Children practise running along, kicking a football from the white line and shooting the ball into the net. After a couple of minutes, blow a whistle for half-time. Children keep count of the goals they score in each half by making a tally on individual whiteboards and adding up their final score.

Things to ask

I wonder how you knew how many goals you scored in the first half?

Did you score more goals in the first half or the second half?

What is the best way to work out how many goals someone scored altogether?

Look, listen, note

Which children can

- use a system for recording each goal?
- find their total score by counting or adding?
- use the vocabulary of calculation?

Challenge

Children use a number line to record the total score for the whole group.

Children find the difference between the number of goals scored in the two halves.

Words to use

how many?, score, count, how many altogether?, one, two, three ... ten, add, total, one more

Maths learning

Calculating

Knowing that the quantity changes when something is added

Finding the total number in two groups by counting

Using the vocabulary involved in adding

Circuit training

Set up a circuit with climbing equipment, tunnel, benches, hoops for jumping in and cones for weaving through. Children work in pairs, using a one-minute sand timer to time how far round the circuit they can get. Children have as many attempts as they wish. Emphasise that improving their own distance for a personal best is more important than trying to beat others.

You need

- Climbing equipment
- Tunnel, benches, hoops, cones
- Sand timers

Things to ask

How far round the circuit did you get?

Which route will you take?

How many minutes do you think it will take to go round the whole circuit?

Look, listen, note

Which children can

- use the sand timers effectively?
- describe their route using positional language?
- use the language of time?

Challenge

Children use alternative ways to time how long it takes to do the whole circuit.

Children record the fastest route round the circuit.

Words to use

over, under, through, up, down, timing, distance, fast, faster slow, slower, timer, minute

Maths learning

Shape and space and measures

Measuring time using a non-standard unit

Using positional language

Using the language of time

Lifting weights

Make up three bags: a pillowcase filled with foam pieces, a very small bag filled with rice and a medium-size bag containing wooden bricks. Make sure the bags are tightly tied. Ask the children to decide which bag is the heaviest. Suggest the children make their own light and heavy bags. Resource the area with a range of small weights such as grams and kilograms. In addition, provide balance scales, small bags and boxes, together with filling materials of rice, sand, pasta and woodchips as well as scoops.

You need

- Three filled bags of different weights
- A range of small weights
- Various empty small bags and boxes
- Filling materials such as rice, sand, pasta, woodchips, cotton-wool balls
- Scoops
- Balance scales
- Weighing materials such as small bricks, conkers, plastic cubes

Things to ask

How can we find out which bag is the lightest?

I wonder how we can make that bag heavier?

Who can explain how to use the balance scales?

Look, listen, note

Which children can

- suggest which bag is the heaviest?
- discuss ways of using balance scales?
- using the language of weight?

Challenge

Children put the three made-up bags in order of weight.

Children make up their own three bags and label them 'heavy', 'heavier', 'heaviest'.

Words to use

full, empty, half full, balance, more, less, heavy, heavier, heaviest, light, lighter, lightest

Maths learning

Measures

Working with variations in size and weight

Using language such as 'heavier' and 'lighter' to compare weights

Ordering two items by weight

Building site

Building sites are always popular and have great scope for developing high-level play. One of the best ways of developing and using maths skills is to build large constructions, handle a wide range of tools with different properties and purposes and use a variety of resources. An outdoor building site will provide opportunities for children to count and sort, use measuring equipment and do estimations.

Maths learning chart

Maths content

Activities	Page	Number	Calculating	Shape and space	Measures	Problem solving
Sandbags	92	✽				✽
The matching tools game	93	✽		✽		✽
Playing pendulums	94		✽			✽
Waterlogged	95		✽		✽	✽
Making clay bricks	96			✽	✽	✽
Building sandcastles	97				✽	✽

Problem solving identified

Activities

Problem solving	Sandbags	The matching tools game	Playing pendulums	Waterlogged	Making clay bricks	Building sand castles
Solving problems	✽		✽	✽	✽	✽
Representing	✽		✽	✽		
Decision making		✽			✽	✽
Reasoning		✽				
Communicating	✽		✽	✽		

Making the most of your building workshop

Resourcing the workshop

Encourage the group to help collect resources for the building workshop: sand tray, wet and dry digging materials such as trowels and buckets, sieves, scoops, tweezers; water tray with drainpipes, plastic guttering, cardboard tubes; workbench with woodworking tools, saws, nails, pliers, screwdrivers, hammers, balsa wood, planks, large log to hammer in nails, duct tape, string; wheelbarrows; builder's trays, pulleys, ropes, real bricks, crates, cardboard boxes; builder's hats, goggles, toolboxes, aprons; desk and telephone, calendar.

Developing a learning conversation

Can you tell me about the plans you have drawn?

What did you notice about the tall tower?

What will you need to make a chair for the bear?

Using ICT to support maths

Torches to look underneath constructions

Mobile phone to find out where the resources are

Electronic measure to find out the size of the building

Maths toolkit

Measuring tapes, large dice, clipboards, balance scales, calculator

Books to read

Fix-it Duck by Jez Alborough (Picture Lions)

The Three Little Pigs (traditional tale)

This is the House that Jack Built by Taback Simms (Puffin)

Henry builds a Cabin by Donald B Johnson (Houghton Mifflin)

Music to listen to

If I had a hammer by Pete Seeger

Violin concerto No 1 by Max Bruch

Songs to sing

Peter hammers with one hammer

The house that Jack built

Humpty Dumpty

London Bridge is falling down

Sandbags

Children make a number line of sandbags. They use a scoop to fill the bags with sand and fix a sticky label onto the bag saying how many scoops are in the bag. When all the bags are labelled, the children put them in order and peg them onto a washing line.

You need

- 10 assorted bags of various sizes
- Dry sand
- Scoops
- Sticky labels
- A washing line and pegs

Things to ask

How will you remember how many scoops you put in that bag?

What number bag do you need to peg up next?

I wonder which bag has the most scoops in?

Look, listen, note

Which children can

- count the number of scoops in the bags?
- recognise the number on the bags?
- put the bags in the right order?

Challenge

Instead of using bags, children make a line of socks containing counting bricks.

Children find something that weighs more than one of the bags.

Words to use

one, two, three … ten, how many?, altogether, number

Maths learning

Number

Saying and using number names

Counting to 10

Recognising numerals to 10

The matching tool game

Photocopy some real tools. Children take it in turns to select a tool from the toolbox and decide if they can match it to one of the six tools on a photocopied sheet. If they can, they keep it; if not, they put it back in the box. The first child to match all their tools is the winner, and they then help everyone else match their tools.

Things to ask

How can you find out how many more tools you need to match?

Why did you decide to take that tool from the box?

Can you think of a way of describing the shape of that tool?

Look, listen, note

Which children can

- use counting to find the total number of tools?
- use number language in discussion?
- recognise the shape outlines of the tools?

Challenge

Children stick number labels on the tools, roll a dice and pick up the tool with that number on.

Put the tools in a feely bag instead of a toolbox.

Words to use

one, two, three ... six, how many?, match, same as, shape, straight, curved

Maths learning

Number and shape and space

Saying and using number names

Counting reliably to six objects

Matching shapes and outlines

Playing pendulums

Make a pendulum by filling a screw-top plastic jar half full of rice or pasta. Tie a long length of string around the neck of the jar and suspend the jar from a tree branch or broom handle attached to a climbing equipment or fence. The children decide where to place the 'skittles' and try to knock them over with the pendulum. They each have two swings of the pendulum and keep score of how many 'skittles' they knock down with each swing.

You need

- A plastic jar
- Rice or pasta
- A 2 metre long length of string
- Five water-filled plastic bottles as skittles
- Pencil, paper, number line, cubes for keeping score

Things to ask

I wonder where the best place is to put the 'skittles'?

Did you knock down more with your first or second swing?

How will you work out how many bottles you knocked down altogether?

Look, listen, note

Which children can

- use a system for recording how many bottles they knocked down?
- find their total score by counting or adding?
- use the vocabulary of calculation?

Challenge

Children number the bottles and score each swing.

Increase the number of bottles to 10.

Words to use

one, two, three ... ten, how many?, count, more, fewer, one more, one less, score, total

Maths learning

Calculating

Knowing that the quantity changes when something is added

Finding the total number in two groups by counting

Using the vocabulary involved in adding

Waterlogged

In this game, children try to fill up all 10 pots with water. In pairs, they collect 10 small pots and fill five with water. They take it in turns to spin the spinner. If the spinner stops on 'empty', they empty out one of the containers into the jug. If it stops on 'full', they fill up one of the containers from the jug. Together, they try to fill all the containers.

Things to ask

How do you know how many full containers you have got?

Would we still have the same number of empty containers if you rearranged them?

What number do you think we will have if you add one more?

Look, listen, note

Can the children

- compare the number of full and empty containers?
- refer to 'more', 'less' and 'the same' in their discussions?
- count 'one more' and 'one less' accurately?

Challenge

Children play the game again and try to empty out all the containers.

Children find a way of recording the results after three spins of the arrow.

Words to use

one, two, three ... ten, how many?, how many altogether?, total, more, fewer, less, most, full, empty

Maths learning

Calculating and measures

Comparing two groups of objects

Using the vocabulary involved in measurement

Finding 'one more' and 'one less'

Making clay bricks

Encourage children to look carefully at some real-house bricks and discuss the shape and feel of them. Each child then takes some clay and moulds a few bricks, using their hands as well as a damp sponge and clay tools. They leave the bricks to dry and harden.

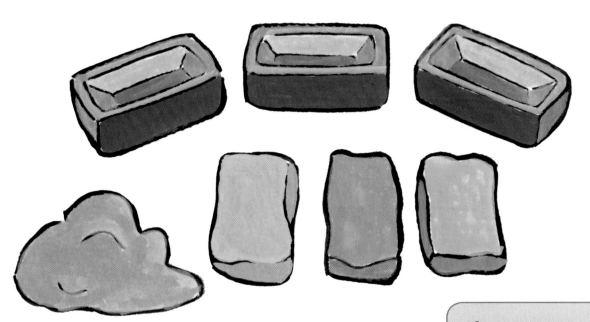

Things to ask

What can you say about one of the bricks?

How much clay will you need?

What is the best way to make the sides straight?

Look, listen, note

Which children can

- identify any shapes correctly?
- identify any similarities between the bricks?
- compare the lengths of the bricks?

Challenge

Children build a brick wall using the bricks they made.

Children make rubbings of brick-wall patterns.

Words to use

large, small, rectangle, square, cuboid, long, longer, longest, short, shorter, shortest, straight, curved

Maths learning

Shape and space and measures

Using mathematical names for 2D shapes and 3D solids

Discussing sameness and difference about shapes

Using the language of length

Building sandcastles

Suggest the group use different-sized containers to make a row of sandcastles with damp sand. Ask the children to decide which castle is the tallest and which castle is the shortest in the row. They vote by putting a red brick next to the tallest castle and a green brick next to the shortest castle. The whole group discusses the results and decides where to put the tallest and shortest labels.

You need

- Damp sand
- Several different-sized containers
- Small spades
- Two labels saying 'tallest and 'shortest'
- Two bricks (red and green) for each child
- Measuring tapes, ribbons, rulers, cubes

Things to ask

Who has an idea how we can find out which castle is the tallest?
Can anyone estimate which is the shortest castle?
What did you notice about the castles?

Look, listen, note

Which children can

- suggest ways of measuring a castle?
- identify any other properties of one of the castles?
- identify and label the castles correctly?

Challenge

Organise a vote to decide which is the children's favourite castle.

Children use shells, flags, buttons and counters to decorate the castles.

Words to use

tall, taller, tallest, short, shorter, shortest, first, second, third

Maths learning

Measures

Categorising objects according to shape or size

Talking about how objects are same or different

Ordering two or three items by height

Real world

Children's play will benefit hugely from having an outdoor role-play area. Children can involve the home corner, travelling between the two areas, giving directions and making maps. A real-world workshop is an area where parents and families can contribute their experiences, thus helping children practise making decisions and communicating as well as counting and calculating.

Maths learning chart

Maths content

Activities	Page	Number	Calculating	Shape and space	Measures	Problem solving
Train driver	100	❀				❀
Racing driver	101	❀				❀
Marine biologist	102		❀			❀
Jewel collector	103		❀			❀
Clothes designer	104			❀	❀	❀
Archaeologist	105	❀		❀		❀

Problem solving identified

Activities

Problem solving	Train driver	Racing driver	Marine biologist	Jewel collector	Clothes designer	Archaeologist
Solving problems		❀	❀	❀	❀	
Representing					❀	
Decision making		❀	❀	❀	❀	❀
Reasoning						❀
Communicating	❀				❀	

Making the most of your real-world role play

Resourcing for real-world role play

Encourage the group to help collect role-play resources: labelled dressing-up clothes boxes; mirror; labelled boxes of role-play props such as artefacts, posters, books; crates, divider, fabrics to create areas; telephone, cash register, paper, pens, signs.

Developing a learning conversation

Can you suggest how to get to the swimming pool?

What would happen if we filled the bucket to the top?

How could we find out how long the stick is?

Using ICT to support maths

Electronic cash till to become a shopkeeper

Calculator to become a banker

Programmable toys to be a map maker

Maths toolkit

Measuring tapes, number cards, money, clock, stopwatches, sand timers

Books to read

Terrific Trains by Tony Mitton and Ant Parker (Kingfisher)

Amazing Aeroplanes by Tony Mitton and Ant Parker (Kingfisher)

Olivia Saves the Circus by Ian Falconer (Simon & Schuster)

Songs to sing

Miss Polly had a dolly who was sick, sick, sick

Please, Mr Crocodile

Music to listen to

Meyong Meyong (Balafon music from Cameroon) by Noah Messomo

Aaj hamaare dil mein from the Bollywood film *Hum aapke hain kaun (What am I to You?)*

Train driver

In a train station role-play area, everyone in the group, has five pennies and sits in a circle, except for one child wearing the train driver's hat in the centre of the circle. The group chooses a number less than 10. They start from 1, counting round the group, and whoever says the 'chosen' number gives a penny to the train driver. The child giving the penny starts the count from 1 again. Children continue until the train driver has collected five pennies. The train driver then changes place with another child in the group, and the group selects another number to be the 'chosen' number.

Things to ask

How many pennies have you collected altogether?

Can anyone remember what the 'chosen' number is this time?

I wonder how many pennies everyone has?

Look, listen, note

Which children can

- recite the number names in the correct order?
- count their collection of pennies and say how many they have?
- remember the chosen number?

Challenge

Children play the game again, choosing a number to 15.

Each child counts how many pennies they have left at the end of the game and decides whether it is more of less than they started with.

Words to use

one, two, three ..., how many altogether?, count, count on, number

Maths learning

Number

Counting aloud in ones

Counting to five objects, saying one number name for each item

Saying and using number names in order

Racing driver

In a garage role-play area, set up a circular road system by drawing a road track on a large sheet of paper. Divide the track into 10 spaces and stick numbers from 1 to 6 on six toy cars to race round the track. Line up the cars on the start line. Children take it in turns to roll a 1–6 dice and move that numbered car one space along the track.

You need

- A drawn circular road track divided into 10 spaces
- Six toy cars numbered 1 to 6
- A 1–6 dice

Things to ask

What number car do you need to move?

How many cars are in the race?

How can we tell who wins the race?

Look, listen, note

Which children can

- recognise the numerals on the car?
- identify which car they need to move?
- move along the track accurately?

Challenge

Children play the game again, racing round the track twice.

Children use 1–6 number cards to decide what car to move and roll the dice to find out many spaces to move.

Words to use

one, two, three ... six, start, finish, number, dice, number pattern

Maths learning

Number

Recognising numerals to 6

Matching a dice-spot arrangement with a numeral

Counting actions

Marine biologist

Children use small aquarium nets to catch plastic sea creatures that are in a large fish tank or water tray. They analyse what creatures they have netted and sort them into a sorting tray. When they have categorised, counted and discussed the creatures, children put them back into the tank.

You need

- A large selection of plastic sea creatures including fish, crabs, sea horses, in a fish tank or water tray
- An aquarium net for each child
- Sorting trays

Things to ask

Why do you think you have more fish than sea horses?

Can you guess how many dolphins you have got altogether?

How can we find out the total number of fish you collected?

Look, listen, note

Which children can

- sort the creatures into different groups?
- discuss differences between each group?
- use the language of calculation?

Challenge

Children record the results of each sorting and compare the differences.

Children re-sort the sea creatures, using different criteria.

Words to use

one, two, three ... ten, how many?, total, more, less, fewer, altogether, same, different, sort

Maths learning

Calculating

Classifying by organising and arranging

Knowing that a group of things changes when something is added

Using language such as 'more' or 'less'

Jewel collector

Arrange a collection of costume jewellery, beads and gems on a large piece of velvet. Give children magnifying lenses to examine the jewels. They then take it in turns to choose a number card and put that many jewels in each box. The next child changes the number of jewels in the boxes according to the number on their card by either removing some jewels or adding to the collection. When the game is over, children choose a soft toy to dress in jewels.

Things to ask

How many jewels are in each of the boxes?

Do you need to take some jewels away or add some?

How can you find out how many jewels there are altogether?

Look, listen, note

Which children can

- use words such as 'more' or 'less' when playing the game?
- work out how many more or fewer jewels they need to put in the box?
- suggest ways of finding a total?

Challenge

Children start with a larger number of jewels and jewellery boxes.

Children use 1–8 number cards.

Words to use

one, two three … five, how many?, more, less, altogether, add, take

Maths learning

Calculating

Comparing two groups of objects

Adding and taking away from a group of objects

Counting out objects from a larger group

Clothes designer

Children choose from a collection of soft toys and play people to make a party outfit for the toy. They measure and make patterns by drawing round the outline of the toy. Children choose the material, cut out and glue fabric to make the outfit. At the end, the children sell the clothes in their dress shop.

Things to ask

Why do you think the material is not long enough?

Can you explain how you made the scarf for Teddy?

What shape did you decide to cut out?

Look, listen, note

Can the children

- describe the order in which they made the outfit?
- use measurement words?
- name they shapes they are using?

Challenge

Children draw diagrams to show how to make a party outfit.

Children write price tickets for the outfits.

Archaeologist

Create a swamp in a builder's tray, using moss, twigs and small plants. Lay a track across the swamp, using 10 small circles made from modelling clay, and put three small clay dog-biscuit bone shapes on each circle. Children roll a 1–3 dice to move play people across the swamp and pick up a bone from any circle they land on. When they have crossed the swamp, children use the bones to make shape outlines.

Things to ask

What shapes did you make?

How many bones have you collected?

Who has the most bones altogether?

Look, listen, note

Can the children

- identify the various shape outlines?
- count along the track the number shown by the dice?
- count accurately the number of bones they have collected?

Challenge

Children use a 1–6 dice and more bones to play the game again.

Children make more complex shape outlines with the collected bones.

Words to use

one, two, three ..., how many?, how many altogether?, count, collect, what number?, most, fewer, shape, triangle, square, rectangle

Maths learning

Number and shape and space

Counting to 10 objects

Using language to compare two quantities

Making patterns with 2D shapes

Working towards the early learning goals in problem solving, reasoning and numeracy

Early learning goal	Small-world workshop						Art space						Newsroom						Magic house						Lib[rary]	
	Going on an outing	Frogs in the pond	Sharing in pairs	Feely-bag-line-up	Making an animal house	Freezing cold dinosaurs	Wall hangings	Revealing	Rolling flowers	Mirror designs	Metal sculptures	Ice-cube painting	Number reference rolls	Glitter calculations	Calculator numbers	Paper-clip chains	Projecting shapes games	Daily news	Red Riding Hood's journey	Rehousing the Three Little Pigs	Jack's beans	The shoemaker's card game	Gingerbread people	Furnishing Bear's house	Book titles	Moving books
Say and use number names in order in familiar contexts	●	●					●						●		●				●	●			●		●	●
Count reliably to 10 everyday objects	●	●				●								●		●			●	●					●	●
Recognise numerals 1 to 9		●												●						●					●	
Begin to use the vocabulary involved in adding and subtracting			●	●			●						●		●											
Use language such as 'more' or 'less' to compare two numbers			●	●											●				●	●						
Find 'one more' or 'one less' than a number from 1 to 10				●					●					●												
Begin to relate addition to combining two groups and subtraction to 'taking away'		●									●					●										
Use language to compare two quantities						●	●	●															●	●	●	
Talk about, recognise and recreate patterns										●	●	●								●						
Use language to describe the shape and size of flat shapes and solids					●	●			●	●	●	●					●								●	●
Use everyday words to describe position		●									●	●										●				
Use developing mathematical ideas and methods to solve practical problems	●	●	●	●	●	●	●	●	●	●	●	●	●	●	●	●	●	●	●	●	●	●	●	●	●	●

This chart identifies the activities and experiences in *Maths Inside and Out* which will support children's developing maths knowledge, skills and understanding so that they can achieve the early learning goals in problem solving, reasoning and numeracy in the Early Years Foundation Stage curriculum.

	Explorer's workshop						Horticulture						Theatre						Vehicle stop						Sports centre						Building site						Real world					
	Pizza picture boxes	Car construction	Fridge magnet designs	Peg lines	Lid rescue	Serving pasta	The seed game	Surveying minibeasts	Sowing sunflowers	Sorting everything	The potato-picking game	Pairing up wellies	Musical instruments	Number dance	The accessory game	Superheroes dressing-up game	Scenery makers	Spectacle masks	The toll gate	Cycling routes	Obstacle course	Key search	Shape deliveries	Wet-tyre printing	Pathway hop	Sorting out the balls	Ten-pin bowling	Goals	Circuit training	Lifting weights	Sandbags	The matching tools	Playing pendulums	Waterlogged	Making clay bricks	Building sandcastles	Train driver	Racing driver	Marine biologist	Jewel collector	Clothes designer	Archaeologist
	●	●									●	●		●											●	●					●	●					●					
	●		●				●	●	●	●	●			●					●						●	●					●	●					●	●				●
	●													●	●				●	●					●	●					●						●					
			●						●	●					●						●	●					●	●					●							●		
																●											●	●					●	●					●	●		
																●																		●								
		●	●						●	●				●							●	●					●	●											●	●		
		●		●	●	●			●					●	●	●	●	●						●						●			●	●	●	●			●		●	●
				●																																						●
										●													●								●				●	●				●		
																		●	●									●														
	●	●	●	●	●	●	●	●	●	●	●	●	●	●	●	●	●	●	●	●	●	●	●	●	●	●	●	●	●	●	●	●	●	●	●	●	●	●	●	●	●	●